Mariko,

   I hope you enjoy the thoughts and feelings expressed in this book. Enjoy your time at BYU-Hawaii - study hard, continue to question and study so your testimony will continue to grow & mature

     Good Luck

          Ben Sarrick

PEACE

PEACE

ESSAYS OF HOPE AND ENCOURAGEMENT

DESERET BOOK COMPANY
SALT LAKE CITY, UTAH

Library of Congress Cataloging-in-Publication Data

Peace.
    p.   cm.
   ISBN 1-57345-271-8
   1. Peace—Religious aspects—Church of Jesus Christ of Latter-day
Saints. 2. Church of Jesus Christ of Latter-day Saints—Doctrines.
I. Deseret Book Company.
BX8643.P43P43   1998
261.8'73—dc21   98-12794
                                            CIP

Printed in the United States of America   18961-6276

10 9   8   7   6   5   4   3   2   1

CONTENTS

Contents

PART 1

PEACE THROUGH CHRIST

THE HEALING POWER OF CHRIST

PRESIDENT GORDON B. HINCKLEY

Recently we were in the city of Bacolod on the island of Negros Occidente, in the Republic of the Philippines. There, to my great surprise, I met a man I had not seen in years.

The weather was steamy hot, as it always is in Bacolod, the center of the once thriving Filipino sugar industry. My friend was in a short-sleeved white shirt with dark trousers, his shoes shined. His beautiful wife, Marva, was beside him. I said, "Victor Jex, what are you doing here?"

He smiled and replied, "We're doing the Lord's work. We're helping the people. We're missionaries."

"Where do you live?"

"In a little house in IloIlo on the island of Panay. We came over on the ferry for the conference."

I thought of when I had last seen them. It was a few years ago. They then lived in a beautiful home in Scarsdale, New York. He was a widely recognized and honored chemist, with a doctorate in chemical engineering. He worked for one of the big multinational companies headquartered in New York. He was credited with putting together the chemical ingredients of a product now sold around the world, the name of which is known to millions of people and the profit from which has run into many millions of dollars for his company.

He was well paid and highly respected.

He was also the president of the Yorktown Stake of The Church of Jesus Christ of Latter-day Saints. He had under his direction a corps of church workers who served faithfully in their local wards, many of whom commuted each day to and from New York City, where they held high and responsible positions in some of the great corporations of America. He was their church leader.

Now he was retired. He and his wife had sold their beautiful home, had given their children what furniture they wanted, and donated the rest to others. They had disposed of their cars and everything except their clothing, their family photographs, and their family history records. They had made themselves available to the Lord and His Church to go wherever they might be sent at their own expense. They were now in the Philippines Bacolod Mission, working among the wonderful, friendly, brown-skinned people of the area. Unemployment is high in this region, and there is much of misery. But wherever Elder and Sister Jex go, they touch for good the lives of those among whom they serve.

They are there to heal the suffering people, to teach the gospel of Christ, to give encouragement and strength and hope and faith. They are there to heal wounds of misunderstanding and contention. They are there to bless the sick and to help those with diseased bodies and frustrated minds. Their smile is infectious, their laugh a joy to hear. They are living humbly among the poor, down at the level of the people, but standing straight and tall to lift with strong hands.

This former New York executive and his charming companion are in the service of the Savior, giving their full time, their resources, and their love to bless with healing the lives of many who are discouraged and need help. Here is a retired New

Yorker, a man of great learning and recognized capacity, living in a home with few conveniences, a simple little place that would fit in the living room of his former house.

He and his wife are there, with others of their kind. They are two of a band of remarkable and dedicated older missionary couples who minister to the wants of people with numerous problems. They receive no financial compensation. They pay their own way. This world's goods mean little to them. As I noted, they sold all they had when they left to come to the Philippines. They will stay for as long as they are assigned by the Church to do so. Then they want to go on another mission. They are healers among the people, serving in the cause of the Master Healer.

I have since reflected much on the power of Christ to heal and bless. It was He who said, "I am come that they might have life, and that they might have it more abundantly." (John 10:10.) In a world of sickness and sorrow, of tension and jealousy and greed, there must be much of healing if there is to be life abundant.

The prophet Malachi declared, "Unto you that fear my name shall the Sun of righteousness arise with healing in his wings." (Mal. 4:2.)

Malachi's prophecy was fulfilled. Jesus came to earth, the Son of God, with power over life and death. He healed the sick, opened the eyes of the blind, caused the lame to walk, and the dead to rise. He was the man of miracles who "went about doing good." (Acts 10:38.)

"So Jesus came again into Cana of Galilee. . . . And there was a certain nobleman, whose son was sick at Capernaum.

"When he heard that Jesus was come out of Judaea into Galilee, he went unto him, and besought him that he would come down, and heal his son: for he was at the point of death. . . .

"Jesus saith unto him, Go thy way; thy son liveth. And the

5

man believed the word that Jesus had spoken unto him, and he went his way.

"And as he was now going down, his servants met him, and told him, saying, Thy son liveth." (John 4:46–47, 50–51.)

This, the second miracle wrought by the Master, was followed by other miracles of healing.

Christ healed by the power of God which was within Him. That power He gave to His chosen disciples, saying, "And I will give unto thee the keys of the kingdom of heaven." (Matt. 16:19.)

That same power has been restored in this generation. It came through the laying on of hands by Peter, James, and John, who received it from the Lord Himself. It was bestowed upon Joseph Smith, the prophet of this dispensation. Its presence is among us. Many of you are acquainted with the history of the Church and are familiar with the account related by Wilford Woodruff concerning the events of July 22, 1839. It is worthy of repetition. Nauvoo at that time was an unhealthy and swampy place. There was much of sickness. Joseph was among those who were afflicted. But being filled with the Spirit, he rose from his bed and went out among the sick, healing them and raising them. He then crossed the river to the settlement in Montrose, Iowa. I quote now from the account of Elder Woodruff:

> The first house he visited was that occupied by Elder Brigham Young, the president of the quorum of the twelve, who lay sick. Joseph healed him, then he arose and accompanied the Prophet on his visit to others who were in the same condition. They visited Elder W. Woodruff, also Elders Orson Pratt and John Taylor, all of whom were living in Montrose. They also accompanied him. The next place they visited was the home of Elijah Fordham, who was supposed to be about breathing his last. When the company entered the room the Prophet of God walked up to the dying man, and took hold of his right hand and spoke to him; but Brother Fordham was unable to speak, his eyes were set in

his head like glass, and he seemed entirely unconscious of all around him. Joseph held his hand and looked into his eyes in silence for a length of time. A change in the countenance of Brother Fordham was soon perceptible to all present. His sight resumed, and upon Joseph asking him if he knew him, he, in a low whisper, answered, "Yes." Joseph asked him if he had faith to be healed. He answered, "I fear it is too late; if you had come sooner I think I would have been healed." The Prophet said, "Do you believe in Jesus Christ?" He answered in a feeble voice, "I do." Joseph then stood erect, still holding his hand in silence several moments; then he spoke in a very loud voice, saying: "Brother Fordham, I command you in the name of Jesus Christ to arise from this bed and be made whole." His voice was like the voice of God, and not of man. It seemed as though the house shook to its very foundations. Brother Fordham arose from his bed and was immediately made whole. His feet were bound in poultices, which he kicked off, then putting on his clothes, he ate a bowl of bread and milk, and followed the Prophet into the street. (Joseph Fielding Smith, *Essentials in Church History,* rev. ed. [Salt Lake City: Deseret Book Co., 1979], pp. 223–24.)

Declared James of old: "Is any sick among you? let him call for the elders of the church; and let them pray over him, anointing him with oil in the name of the Lord: And the prayer of faith shall save the sick, and the Lord shall raise him up; and if he have committed sins, they shall be forgiven him." (James 5:14–15.)

That power to heal the sick is still among us. It is the power of the priesthood of God. It is the authority held by the elders of this Church.

We welcome and praise and utilize the marvelous procedures of modern medicine which have done so much to alleviate human suffering and lengthen human life. All of us are indebted to the dedicated men and women of science and medicine who have conquered so much of disease, who have mitigated pain, who have stayed the hand of death. I cannot say enough of gratitude for them.

Yet they are the first to admit the limitations of their knowledge and the imperfection of their skills in dealing with many matters of life and death. The mighty Creator of the heavens and the earth and all that in them are has given to His servants a divine power that transcends all the powers and knowledge of men. I venture to say that there is scarcely a faithful elder within the sound of my voice who could not recount instances in which this healing power has been made manifest in behalf of the sick. It is the healing power of Christ.

And there is much of sickness among us other than that of the body.

There is the sickness of sin. One of our national magazines carried an extensive review of a sacrilegious film being shown in theaters across the world. Letters poured in to the editor. I quote from one of these. Said the writer, "I am a former alcoholic and adulterer set free by the power of the living Jesus Christ." (*Time,* 5 Sept. 1988, p. 7.)

Legion are those who have testified of the healing power of Christ to lift them from the desolation of sin to higher and nobler living.

There is much of another category of sickness among us. I speak of conflicts, quarrels, arguments which are a debilitating disease particularly afflicting families. If there be such problems in the homes of any reading these words, I encourage you to invite the healing power of Christ. To those to whom He spoke on the Mount, Jesus said:

"Ye have heard that it hath been said, An eye for an eye, and a tooth for a tooth: But I say unto you, That ye resist not evil: but whosoever shall smite thee on thy right cheek, turn to him the other also. . . . And whosoever shall compel thee to go a mile, go with him twain." (Matt. 5:38–39, 41.)

The application of this principle, difficult to live but wondrous in its curative powers, would have a miraculous effect on our troubled homes. It is selfishness which is the cause of most of our misery. It is as a cankering disease. The healing power of Christ, found in the doctrine of going the second mile, would do wonders to still argument and accusation, faultfinding and evil speaking.

The same healing spirit would do wonders for the sickness of our society. The Lord has declared that it is our duty, as those blessed with the healing power of the Master, to "succor the weak, lift up the hands which hang down, and strengthen the feeble knees." (D&C 81:5.)

Great is the healing capacity of those who follow the admonition given by James: "Pure religion and undefiled before God and the Father is this, To visit the fatherless and widows in their affliction, and to keep himself unspotted from the world." (James 1:27.)

We live in an environment where there is much of litigation and conflict, of suing and countersuing. Even here the powers of healing may be invoked. As a young man I worked with Elder Stephen L Richards, then of the Council of the Twelve. When he came into the First Presidency of the Church, he asked me to assist him with a very delicate and sensitive matter. It was fraught with most grave and serious consequences. After listening to him discuss it, I said, "President Richards, you don't want me; you want a lawyer." He said, "I am a lawyer. I don't want to litigate this. I want to compose it."

We directed our efforts to that end, and wonderful results followed. Money was saved, much of it. Embarrassment was avoided. The work was moved forward without fanfare or headlines. Wounds were closed. The healing powers of the Master, the principles of the gospel of Jesus Christ, were invoked in a delicate and difficult situation to compose what otherwise could have become a catastrophe.

It is not always easy to live by these doctrines when our very natures impel us to fight back. For instance, there are those who have made it the mission of their lives to try to destroy this, the work of God. It has been so from the beginning of the Church, and now, in recent times, we are seeing more of it with evil accusations, falsehoods, and innuendo designed to embarrass this work and its officers. A natural inclination is to fight back, to challenge these falsehoods and bring action against their perpetrators. But when these inclinations make themselves felt, there arise also the words of the Master Healer, who said:

"Ye have heard that it hath been said, Thou shalt love thy neighbour, and hate thine enemy.

"But I say unto you, Love your enemies, bless them that curse you, do good to them that hate you, and pray for them which despitefully use you, and persecute you." (Matt. 5:43–44.)

Most of us have not reached that stage of compassion and love and forgiveness. It is not easy. It requires a self-discipline almost greater than we are capable of. But as we try, we come to know that there is a resource of healing, that there is a mighty power of healing in Christ, and that if we are to be His true servants we must not only exercise that healing power in behalf of others, but, perhaps more important, inwardly.

I would that the healing power of Christ might spread over the earth and be diffused through our society and into our homes, that it might cure men's hearts of the evil and adverse elements of greed and hate and conflict. I believe it could happen. I believe it must happen. If the lamb is to lie down with the lion, then peace must overcome conflict, healing must mend injury.

Jesus of Nazareth healed the sick among whom He moved.

His regenerating power is with us today to be invoked through His holy priesthood. His divine teachings, His incomparable example, His matchless life, His all-encompassing sacrifice will bring healing to broken hearts, reconciliation to those who argue and shout, even peace to warring nations if sought with humility and forgiveness and love.

As members of the Church of Jesus Christ, ours is a ministry of healing, with a duty to bind the wounds and ease the pain of those who suffer. Upon a world afflicted with greed and contention, upon families distressed by argument and selfishness, upon individuals burdened with sin and troubles and sorrows, I invoke the healing power of Christ, giving my witness of its efficacy and wonder. I testify of Him who is the great source of healing. He is the Son of God, the Redeemer of the world, "The Sun of Righteousness," who came "with healing in his wings." (Mal. 4:2.)

President Gordon B. Hinckley was called as a General Authority in 1958, was ordained an Apostle in 1961, and was sustained as President of the Church in 1995.

PEACE IN THIS WORLD

PRESIDENT MARION G. ROMNEY

In the fifty-ninth section of the Doctrine and Covenants we read:

"He who doeth the works of righteousness shall receive his reward, even peace in this world, and eternal life in the world to come." (D&C 59:23.)

This text promises two rewards: one in this world and another in the world to come. Reference to "the world to come" brings to mind an incident that occurred in a divorce action when I was practicing law some thirty-five years ago. As the court was about to render its decision, the plaintiff, a woman, requested and was granted a private conference. Nervously approaching the bench, she audibly whispered: "Your honor, I want a divorce for this world only, not for the world to come."

Unlike that judge, the Great Judge who spoke the words of our text has jurisdiction both in this world and the world to come; although the promised rewards in the two are interdependent, I propose in these pages to deal principally with peace in *this* world.

First, let us agree upon the meaning of the word "peace." "Freedom from civil disturbance or war" is one dictionary definition. That this is not the "peace" promised, however, is evident from the fact that about the time the Lord spoke our text, he also said: " . . . the hour is not yet, but is nigh at hand, when peace

13

[meaning freedom from civil disturbance or war] shall be taken from the earth" (D&C 1:35), and from the further fact that in 1894 and again in 1896, President Woodruff, then the Lord's mouthpiece on the earth, indicated that the time for such peace to be taken from the earth had then come. (See *Discourses of Wilford Woodruff,* sel. G. Homer Durham [Salt Lake City: Bookcraft, 1946], pp. 251–52.) Informed Latter-day Saints know that this earth will never again, during its telestial existence, be free from civil disturbance and war.

Nor does the "peace" of which we speak mean "harmony in personal relations," another dictionary definition. Jesus made this plain when he said:

"Think not that I am come to send peace on earth: I came not to send peace, but a sword. For I am come to set a man at variance against his father, and the daughter against her mother, and the daughter in law against her mother in law." (Matt. 10:34–35.)

Jesus was, however, talking about the "peace" of which we speak when to his disciples he said:

"Peace I leave with you, my peace I give unto you: not as the world giveth, give I unto you. Let not your heart be troubled, neither let it be afraid." (John 14:27.)

He was also talking about such "peace" when, just before he offered his intercessory prayer, he concluded his instructions to his disciples with the words:

"These things I have spoken unto you, that in me ye might have peace. In the world ye shall have tribulation: but be of good cheer; I have overcome the world." (John 16:33.)

From these scriptures it is apparent that the "peace" of our text is heaven-sent.

Among those who enjoy it, of course, it brings "harmony in personal relations." If men generally enjoyed it, it would banish civil disturbance and war. But in the absence of both mutual concord and civil peace, it may and does dwell in the hearts of many people. The promise of it runs to each and every person who will qualify himself to receive it, regardless of the actions of those about him. "He who doeth the works of righteousness shall," says the Lord—not *may* or *can,* but *shall*—"receive his reward, even peace in this world, and eternal life in the world to come." (D&C 59:23.)

The revelation from which my text is taken not only extends to the Saints the comforting promise of peace in this world; it also specifies some of the specific works of righteousness upon which the promise is conditioned. The circumstances under which the revelation was received, as well as its content, are interesting and instructive.

During the summer of 1831, "the mission to Western Missouri and the gathering of the Saints to that place was the most important subject which then engrossed the attention of the Church." (*History of the Church,* 7 vols., 2d ed. [Salt Lake City: Deseret Book Co., 1967], 1:182.) Those are the words of the Prophet Joseph. Between the 19th of June and the middle of July the Prophet and his associates traveled from Kirtland, Ohio, to Independence, Missouri. The Prophet himself walked all the way from St. Louis to Independence, a distance of about 300 miles.

Between the time of their arrival and the 7th of August, when the revelation was given, the Colesville Branch arrived to join the few Saints who had preceded them. "W. W. Phelps preached to a western audience." (*History of the Church,* 1:190.) Several other revelations were received. "The first log, for a house, as a foundation of Zion in Kaw township" was laid. (*History of the Church,* 1:196.) The site for the temple was revealed and dedicated, and the first conference in Zion was held.

Interest and enthusiasm among the people ran high. The

15

Saints, having but recently arrived on the scene, were all agog over the glorious predictions concerning latter-day Zion.

It was under these circumstances, with the Saints perhaps a little overanxiously anticipating Zion as it shall be in its perfection and without fully appreciating the works of righteousness required to bring about the perfection, that the Lord said to them:

"Blessed . . . are they who have come up unto this land with an eye single to my glory. . . .

"Yea, blessed are they whose feet stand upon the land of Zion, who have obeyed my gospel; for . . .

" . . . they shall . . . be crowned with blessings from above, yea, and with commandments not a few, and with revelations in their time—they that are faithful and diligent before me.

"Wherefore, I give unto them a commandment, saying thus: Thou shalt love the Lord thy God with all thy heart, with all thy might, mind, and strength; and in the name of Jesus Christ thou shalt serve him.

"Thou shalt love thy neighbor as thyself. Thou shalt not steal; neither commit adultery, nor kill, nor do anything like unto it.

"Thou shalt thank the Lord thy God in all things.

"Thou shalt offer a sacrifice unto the Lord thy God in righteousness, even that of a broken heart and a contrite spirit.

"And that thou mayest more fully keep thyself unspotted from the world, thou shalt go to the house of prayer and offer up thy sacraments upon my holy day." (D&C 59:1, 3–9.)

Then, after giving detailed instructions concerning observance of the Sabbath day, the Lord concludes with this promise:

"Learn that he who doeth the works of righteousness shall receive his reward, even peace in this world, and eternal life in the world to come." (D&C 59:23.)

In this manner did the Lord relate the rewards to specific

works and urged the Saints to learn for themselves that peace in this world comes as a reward for works of righteousness.

Peace in this world, being an inner feeling, is difficult to define. It may, therefore, perhaps be best understood through illustrations. You who are familiar with the Book of Mormon will recall the experiences of Enos, who, in the true spirit of repentance, sought forgiveness of sins with such persistent faith and prayer that "there came a voice unto [him,] saying: Enos, thy sins are forgiven thee, and thou shalt be blessed." Whereupon Enos wrote:

"I . . . knew that God could not lie; wherefore, my guilt was swept away.

"And I said: Lord, how is it done?

"And he said unto me: Because of thy faith in Christ, . . . wherefore, go to, thy faith hath made thee whole." (Enos 1:6–8.)

Thereafter Enos besought the Lord to preserve a record, " . . . that it might be brought forth at some future day unto the Lamanites, . . . and he covenanted with me that he would bring them forth unto the Lamanites in his own due time. And I, Enos, knew it would be according to the covenant which he had made; wherefore my soul did rest." (Enos 1:13, 16–17.)

Contributing to the peace and rest that filled the soul of Enos was the accompanying assurance of eternal life in the world to come that accompanied it. This he thus expressed:

"I soon go to the place of my rest, which is with my Redeemer; for I know that in him I shall rest. And I rejoice in the day when my mortal shall put on immortality, and shall stand before him; then shall I see his face with pleasure, and he will say unto me: Come unto me, ye blessed, there is a place prepared for you in the mansions of my Father. Amen." (Enos 1:27.)

At times numerous persons have sought and obtained this feeling of peace at the same time. Recorded in the first chapters of Mosiah is a powerful message received by King Benjamin from

17

an angel of the Lord and delivered by him to his subjects. The message concerned the atonement of Christ, by means of which men, through faith and repentance, may obtain forgiveness of sins, which forgiveness heals the spirit and thus brings peace to the soul. Having delivered the message, Benjamin "cast his eyes round about on the multitude, and behold they had fallen to the earth, for the fear of the Lord had come upon them.

"And they all cried aloud with one voice, saying: O have mercy, and apply the atoning blood of Christ that we may receive forgiveness of our sins, and our hearts may be purified; for we believe in Jesus Christ, the Son of God. . . .

"And it came to pass that after they had spoken these words the Spirit of the Lord came upon them, and they were filled with joy, having received a remission of their sins, and having peace of conscience, because of the exceeding faith which they had in Jesus Christ." (Mosiah 4:1–3.)

Another dramatic example of a community experiencing peace in a world of tribulation concerns the people of Alma, who had covenanted with the Lord in the waters of Mormon and who were later brought into bondage by Amulon, who "put tasks upon them, and put taskmasters over them.

"And . . . so great were their afflictions that they began to cry mightily to God.

"And Amulon commanded them that they should stop their cries; and he put guards over them to watch them, that whosoever should be found calling upon God should be put to death.

"And Alma and his people did not raise their voices to the Lord their God, but did pour out their hearts to him; . . .

"And it came to pass that the voice of the Lord came to them in their afflictions, saying: Lift up your heads and be of good comfort, for I know of the covenant which ye have made unto me; . . .

"And I will . . . ease the burdens which are put upon your

shoulders, that even you cannot feel them upon your backs, . . . while you are in bondage; . . .

"And now it came to pass that the burdens which were laid upon Alma and his brethren were made light; yea, the Lord did strengthen them that they could bear up their burdens with ease, . . .

"And it came to pass that so great was their faith and their patience that the voice of the Lord came unto them again, saying: Be of good comfort, for on the morrow I will deliver you out of bondage." (Mosiah 24:9–16.)

These illustrations are but samples of the many to be found in the scriptures. But each of them, as do the others, evidences the truth that peace in this world always comes after the receiver has done the works of righteousness. Enos, the subjects of King Benjamin, and the people of Alma had all demonstrated, by good works, their faith in Christ before the reward came. This is the way peace comes in this world. It can be obtained in no other way. The promised peace emanates from Christ. He is the source of it. His spirit is the essence of it.

I bear my witness that I know that we may enjoy the promised "peace in this world" and the assurance of "eternal life in the world to come" on the prescribed terms. Only those who experience such peace and assurance can appreciate how they come and the joy they bring. The thought of them, however, is associated in my mind with two scriptures. First from the account Nephi gives of his experience on the mount with the Spirit of the Lord, who said to him:

"Knowest thou the meaning of the tree which thy father saw?

"And I answered him, . . . Yea, it is the love of God, which sheddeth itself abroad in the hearts of the children of men; wherefore, it is the most desirable above all things.

"And he spake unto me, saying: Yea, and the most joyous to the soul." (1 Ne. 11:21–23.)

Now, such joy and peace does not come from knowing about Deity; it comes from the knowledge implied by Jesus when, thanking his Father for the power to give eternal life to his followers, he said: "And this is life eternal, that they might know thee the only true God, and Jesus Christ, whom thou hast sent." (John 17:3.)

God bless you that you may set your sights on coming to know God, the Eternal Father, and Jesus Christ whom he has sent: not just to talk about them, but a personal acquaintance with them. When you get such a knowledge, you will have "peace in this world."

President Marion G. Romney was called to be a General Authority in 1941, was ordained an Apostle in 1951, was called into the First Presidency of the Church in 1972, and died in 1988.

"THE PEACEABLE THINGS OF THE KINGDOM"

ELDER JEFFREY R. HOLLAND

The great Isaiah foresaw the very setting in which the Church now finds itself: "And it shall come to pass in the last days, that the mountain of the Lord's house shall be established in the top of the mountains, and shall be exalted above the hills; and all nations shall flow unto it. And many people shall go and say, Come ye, and let us go up to the mountain of the Lord, to the house of the God of Jacob; and he will teach us of his ways, and we will walk in his paths: for out of Zion shall go forth the law, and the word of the Lord from Jerusalem." (Isa. 2:2–3.)

Of such comforting latter-day direction, including its divine source, Isaiah would go on to say: "How beautiful upon the mountains are the feet of him that bringeth good tidings, that publisheth peace." (Isa. 52:7.)

Peace and good tidings; good tidings and peace. These are among the ultimate blessings that the gospel of Jesus Christ brings a troubled world and the troubled people who live in it, solutions to personal struggles and human sinfulness, a source of strength for days of weariness and hours of genuine despair. The Church of Jesus Christ of Latter-day Saints declares that it is the Only Begotten Son of God Himself who gives us this help and this hope. Such assurance is as "firm as the mountains

21

around us." (See "Carry On," *Hymns,* 1985, no. 255.) As the Book of Mormon prophet Abinadi made clear in a slight variation of Isaiah's exclamation:

"O how beautiful upon the mountains are the feet of him that bringeth good tidings, that is *the founder of peace,* yea, even the Lord, who has redeemed his people; yea, him who has granted salvation unto his people." (Mosiah 15:18; italics added.)

Ultimately it is Christ who is beautiful upon the mountain. And it is His merciful promise of "peace in this world," His good tidings of "eternal life in the world to come" (D&C 59:23) that make us fall at His feet and call His name blessed and give thanks for the restoration of His true and living Church.

This search for peace is one of the ultimate quests of the human soul. We all have highs and lows, but such times come and they usually always go. Kind neighbors assist. Beautiful sunshine brings encouragement. A good night's sleep usually works wonders. But there are times in all of our lives when deep sorrow or suffering or fear or loneliness make us cry out for the peace which only God Himself can bring. These are times of piercing spiritual hunger when even the dearest friends cannot fully come to our aid.

Perhaps you know people in your local ward or your stake—or in your own home—courageous people who are carrying heavy burdens and feeling private pain, who are walking through the dark valleys of this world's tribulation. Some may be desperately worried about a husband or a wife or a child, worried about their health or their happiness or their faithfulness in keeping the commandments. Some are living with physical pain, or emotional pain, or disabilities that come with age. Some are troubled as to how to make ends meet financially—and some ache with the private loneliness of an empty house or an empty room or simply empty arms.

These beloved people seek the Lord and His word with particular urgency, often revealing their true emotions only when the scriptures are opened or the hymns are sung or prayers are offered. Sometimes only then do the rest of us realize they feel near the end of their strength—they are tired in brain and body and heart, they wonder if they can get through another week or another day or sometimes just another hour. They are desperate for the Lord's help and know that in such times of extremity nothing else will do.

Well, at least one of the purposes of the teachings of the prophets down through the ages is to declare to these very people that the Lord is equally fervent in trying to reach them, that when there is trouble His hopes and His striving and His efforts greatly exceed our own and it never ceases.

We have been promised, "He that keepeth [us] will not slumber . . . nor [will he] sleep." (Ps. 121:3–4.)

Christ and His angels and prophets forever labor to buoy up our spirits, steady our nerves, calm our hearts, and send us forth with renewed strength and resolute hope. They wish all to know that "if God be for us, who can be against us?" (Rom. 8:31.) In the world we shall have tribulation, but we are to be of good cheer. Christ has overcome the world. (See John 16:33.) Through His suffering and His obedience He has earned and rightly bears the crown of "Prince of Peace." (Isa. 9:6.)

In that spirit we declare to all the world that for real and abiding peace to come, we must strive to be more like that exemplary Son of God. Many among us are trying to do that. I salute you for your obedience, your forbearance, your waiting faithfully upon the Lord for the strength you seek and which will surely come. Some of us, on the other hand, need to make some changes, need to make greater effort in gospel living. And change we can. The very beauty of the word *repentance* is the promise of escaping old problems and old habits and old sorrows and old sins. It is among the most hopeful and encouraging—and yes, most peaceful—words in the gospel vocabulary. In seeking true peace some of us need to improve what has to be improved, confess what needs to be confessed, forgive what has to be forgiven, and forget what should be forgotten in order that serenity can come to us. If there is a commandment we are breaking, and as a result it is breaking us and hurting those who love us, let us call down the power of the Lord Jesus Christ to help us, to free us, to lead us through repentance to that peace "which passeth all understanding." (Philip. 4:7.)

And when God has forgiven us, which He is so eternally anxious to do, may we have the good sense to walk away from those problems, to leave them alone, to let the past bury the past. If one of you has made a mistake, even a serious mistake, but you have done all you can according to the teachings of the Lord and the governance of the Church to confess it and feel sorrow for it and set it as right as can be, then trust in God, walk into His light, and leave those ashes behind you. Someone once said that repentance is the first pressure we feel when drawn to the bosom of God. For real peace may I recommend an immediate rush to the bosom of God, leaving behind you all that would bring sorrow to your soul or heartache to those who love you. "Depart from evil," the scripture says, "and do good." (Ps. 34:14.)

Closely related to our own obligation to repent is the generosity of letting others do the same—we are to forgive even as we are forgiven. In this we participate in the very essence of the atonement of Jesus Christ. Surely the most majestic moment of that fateful Friday, when nature convulsed and the veil of the temple was rent, was that unspeakably merciful moment when Christ said, "Father, forgive them; for they know not what they do." (Luke 23:34.) As our advocate with the Father, He is still making that same plea today—in your behalf and mine.

Here, as in all things, Jesus set the standard for us to follow. Life is too short to be spent nursing animosities or in keeping a box score of offenses against us—you know—no runs, no hits, all errors. We don't want God to remember our sins; there is something fundamentally wrong in our relentlessly trying to remember those of others.

When we have been hurt, undoubtedly God takes into account what wrongs were done to us and what provocations there are for our resentments, but clearly the more provocation there is and the more excuse we can find for our hurt, all the more reason for us to forgive and be delivered from the destructive hell of such poisonous venom and anger. (Adapted from George Macdonald.) It is one of those ironies of godhood that in order to find peace, the offended as well as the offender must engage the principle of forgiveness.

Yes, peace is a very precious commodity, a truly heartfelt need and there are many things we can do to achieve it. But— for whatever reason—life has its moments when uninterrupted peace may seem to elude us for a season. We may wonder why there are such times in life, particularly when we may be trying harder than we have ever tried to live worthy of God's blessings and His help. When problems or sorrows or sadness come and they *don't* seem to be our fault, what are we to make of their unwelcome appearance?

With time and perspective we recognize that such problems in life do come for a purpose, if only to allow the one who faces such despair to be convinced that he really does need divine strength beyond himself, that she really does need the offer of heaven's hand. Those who feel no need for mercy usually never seek it and almost never bestow it. Those who have never had a heartache or a weakness or felt lonely or forsaken never have had to cry unto heaven for relief of such personal pain. Surely it is better to find the goodness of God and the grace of Christ, even at the price of despair, than to risk living our lives in a moral or material complacency that has never felt any need for faith or forgiveness, any need for redemption or relief.

A life without problems or limitations or challenges—life without "opposition in all things" (2 Ne. 2:11) as Lehi phrased it—would paradoxically but in very fact be less rewarding and ennobling than one which confronts, even frequently confronts, difficulty and disappointment and sorrow. As beloved Eve said, were it not for the difficulties faced in a fallen world, neither she nor Adam nor any of the rest of us ever would have known "the joy of our redemption, and the eternal life which God giveth unto all the obedient." (Moses 5:11.)

So life has its oppositions and its conflicts, and the gospel of Jesus Christ has answers and assurances. In a time of terrible civil warfare, one of the most gifted leaders ever to strive to hold a nation together said what could be said of marriages and families and friendships. Praying for peace, pleading for peace, seeking peace in any way that would not compromise union, Abraham Lincoln said in those dark, dark days of his First Inaugural, "Though passion may have strained, it must not break our bonds of affection. The mystic chords of memory . . . will yet swell . . . when again touched, as surely they will be, by the better angels of our nature." (First Inaugural Address, 4 Mar. 1861.)

The better angels of our nature. That is much of what the Church and the gospel of Jesus Christ are about. The appeal today and tomorrow and forever is to be better, to be cleaner, to be kinder, to be holier; to seek peace and always be believing.

I have personally known in my own life the realization of the promise "that the everlasting God, . . . the Creator of the ends of the earth, fainteth not, neither is [he] weary." I am a witness that "He giveth power to the faint; and to them that have no might he increaseth strength." (Isa. 40:28–29.)

I know that in times of fear or fatigue "they that wait upon the Lord shall renew their strength; they shall mount up with wings as eagles; they shall run, and not be weary; and they shall walk, and not faint." (Isa. 40:31.)

We receive the gift of such majestic might and sanctifying renewal through the redeeming grace of the Lord Jesus Christ. He has overcome the world, and if we will take upon us His name and "walk in His paths" and keep our covenants with Him we shall, ere long, have peace. Such a reward is not only possible, it is certain.

"For the mountains shall depart and the hills be removed, but my kindness shall not depart from thee, neither shall the covenant of my peace be removed, saith the Lord that hath mercy on thee." (3 Ne. 22:10.)

Of Him and His good tidings, of the publication of His peace in this His true Church, and of His living prophet, I bear grateful and joyful witness.

Elder Jeffrey R. Holland was called as a General Authority in 1989, and was ordained an Apostle in 1994.

"THE PEACE WHICH PASSETH UNDERSTANDING"

PRESIDENT SPENCER W. KIMBALL

This is a crucial hour in history. Those now entering adulthood will find that their paths will not be all flowers. There will be hills to climb and ravines to cross. Would that I might place in your hands a light to guide your footsteps in that somewhat bloody march. I have confidence, not only in your ability to cope with the problems of life, but in your steadfastness, dependability, and desire to hold fast to that which is good and worthwhile.

We know that much that occurs in the world is most distressing, but the clouds, though black and threatening, have their silver linings; all is not dark and hopeless; all is not gloom and despair. Joy may still be found, and peace may continue to fill your soul.

As we analyze the chaotic condition of our world, we are shocked and disgusted to know that nations, to settle differences, must kill and starve and poison, and sink to the level of animals, yet it is comforting to know that men may live their individual lives on a higher plane, quite independent of the conditions that prevail about them.

True, the world may bring many bitter disappointments. But if you will it so, life may go on for you full, sweet, and

29

abundant, for the worthwhile things do not change in times of trouble.

Life is full of paradoxes. Can there be love in a world of hatred, suspicion and venom? The Lord said there could. It was in a warring world that He said, "Love your enemies, bless them that curse you, do good to them that hate you, and pray for them which despitefully use you, and persecute you." (Matt. 5:44.)

Can there be peace in a world of mad nations tearing at each others' throats? The Prince of Peace proclaimed from and in such a world, "Peace I leave with you, my peace I give unto you: not as the world giveth, give I unto you. Let not your heart be troubled, neither let it be afraid." (John 14:27.)

His peace, as He said, was not the kind which the world could give, not such a peace as was given the enemy after World War I, which resolved itself into a temporary truce only long enough to prepare for hostilities of the next war. Samuel Butler says: "He that complies against his will is of the same opinion still." But the peace of the Lord would offer a permanent freedom from the troubled heart, and from fear and mental distress.

But regardless of whether there is war or peace in the national life of the peoples of the globe, each of us as individuals may mold his own life into one of selfishness or selflessness; it may be one of honor or dishonor; it may be one of misery or happiness; or it may be governed by fear and agitation, or full of real and enduring peace.

Paul said to the Romans, "For to be carnally minded is death; but to be spiritually minded is life and peace." (Rom. 8:6.)

There can be peace in individual lives in a world of warring nations preparing and engaging in deadly conflict. Was not the Savior Himself born into a world of distress and turmoil, to a people under the yoke of oppression and intolerant and vexatious subjugation? And paradoxically, His advent was heralded by angels voicing a harmonious soul-inspiring symphony: "Glory to God in the highest, and on earth peace, good will toward men." (Luke 2:14.)

Peace means the absence of hostilities, whether they be battles with gun and saber and bomb, or battles with sin and weakness or other inward conflict. Peace means an absence of discord, of moral conflict, of agitating passions and fears.

The outward condition means less and the inward feelings more, for peace comes in triumph from within. Tranquility of soul, joy, and peace are the fruits of right living, nearness to and a dependence upon God, and an assurance of acceptability of one's life and a conviction of the completeness and divinity of the program.

Peace is when you can turn a corner without apprehension and look in the eye those you meet; it is the supremacy over fear, not fearlessness, but the courage to go forward in spite of fear; it is the hearing of the telephone bell without a start; the opening of your door to the police without a quiver; the receiving of a telegram without a tremble.

Peace is when the fracture is knit; when the chasm is bridged; when the villagers come home at night from their fields knowing where they will sleep; when the grain is stored in the barn; the folded linen is piled in the drawer, and the fruit is canned and stored in the cupboard.

Peace is the spirit of a Mormon boy who wrote during wartime:

"I am extremely grateful for the gospel and the understanding it gives me of the purpose of life and of the hereafter. I see my buddies go fearfully and tremblingly into battle and many of them come back on stretchers, others buried in new graves, and I approach the same possible fate with courage and without fear. I would take my place in the eternities, proud of my heritage,

31

fully assured of continuance of life and move into a serener sphere of action without malice or hate or bitterness."

Peace is like standing on a solid rock high above the water after having stood on melting sands lapped by treacherous tides.

Peace is when the world is self-contained. When factories make radios and washers and refrigerators instead of tanks and guns and explosives. And when plows and harvesters are made where U-boats and destroyers were built.

Peace is when destruction ceases and production begins; when maneuver fields are turned by the plow and barracks reconstructed into homes. And when hunger is history, education increased, and every man goes home at night to his family unafraid.

The power of individual peace in a warring world is shown in the following story: During World War II, one of our brethren attended a hotel convention in the East. As part of the preliminaries he was introduced as a delegate from Salt Lake City, Utah. Later a distinguished gentleman approached him and asked if he knew any Mormons out there.

"Yes, I know a few hundred by name," he said, "and I consider myself a fairly good Mormon."

"Would you like to come to my room?" the Eastern gentleman asked. "I have a letter I would like to show you from my son who is a major in the army of North Africa."

The letter was written following the landing on the beachheads of Italy. The major wrote his father that he was in command of one of the landing barges. (It is said that these barges carried between 200 and 300 men.) Preparations had been made and now the barges were actually on their way to the Italian coast. It was a long trip of about twelve hours and the bravado and bluff with which the boys had begun their perilous journey was fast ebbing away. They were becoming nervous, agitated, and full of fear. At this hour of peril their religion was meaning much to them. A line of anxious men lined up at the door of the cabin of the chaplain on the boat to make their confessions and to receive spiritual strength. They were in line waiting their turn for hours. The major continued with his letter:

I noticed one young fellow talking to a small group which continued to grow in number and I joined them to see what he was saying. He was now standing as the crowd increased and he spoke with assurance and power. He was calm, composed, and fearless as he stood those two hours before these men, his companions. I never before saw such composure and peace in one. Never before had I seen one with such self-control, as he talked to those boys facing the unknown perils of the beachheads. Their jitters, their fear, their consternation and dread turned to quiet and assurance as he explained the purposes of life. He told them where they came from, why they were born into this world, and that the spirit was eternal; he told them that life here was not "to eat, drink and be merry" but to learn, and grow and overcome the weaknesses of the flesh and work out an exaltation; and that life was eternal. He admitted that there was likelihood of their failing to come out of this invasion alive, but since life is eternal, there was little difference as to when the transition should come. He explained that if we die in Christ, true to His teachings, we shall not taste of death and it will be sweet to us, and even if their lives were taken, that that would not be the end. They could greet their sweethearts, wives, parents, brothers, and sisters and know and recognize them as such and have joy in greeting them. And when the boy was finished, the change in his listeners was astounding. Fear had been replaced by courage; agitation by composure; uncertainty by faith and hope. The jittery boys were now determined men, calm, set, and ready for what might come. Peace had come to them in this hour and with it strength and courage and hope.

The major continued:

"I wondered where this boy came by such a wholesome philosophy and I went up to him with that question.

"'It is the doctrine of my Church,' the boy answered.

"I asked him where he came from and learned that he was from a small town in southern Utah.

"'Are you a Mormon?' was my next question and he replied:

"'Yes. I am a Mormon and it was Mormon doctrine I was telling them.'

"Father," continued the army major, "there was something about that boy that set him apart from the rest of the fellows, and if I ever come home alive from this war, you and I must go out to Utah and see what kind of people it is who teach such a comprehensive philosophy of life."

What courage! What faith! What a testimony! What peace! Certainly the promise of the Redeemer had been fulfilled in this case: "My peace I give unto you." (John 14:27.) Surely here was that peace which passeth understanding, the peace of God which shall keep your hearts and minds through Jesus Christ.

The harbinger of peace was not accepted nor received by His people, for the brand of peace He offered was not the kind they had been expecting. Long centuries they had looked for a redeemer but their interpretations of the numerous prophecies left them expecting a warrior to lead them victoriously against their political enemies and free them from Roman bondage. Wishful thinking and ambitious hopes had led them to look for a redeemer who would reign with the sword, as a political king, and put under his feet all kingdoms and dominions. "The Prince of Peace," "The Mighty God," "The King of Kings" (Isa. 9:6; 2 Ne. 19:6; 1 Tim. 6:15)—all these meant only one thing to the anticipating Jews. "The government shall be upon his shoulders" (Isa. 9:6) meant to them a Deliverer who would tear from their necks the shackles of hated militaristic Rome for whom the Jewish hatred smoldered and was not quenched.

They read the Psalmist's words—"The Lord will bless his people with peace" (Ps. 29:11) and "He maketh peace in thy borders, and filleth thee with the finest of the wheat" (Ps. 147:14)—and they envisioned a conqueror with metal sword and shining shield leading them into world domination. It meant, at last, military success. Yet such a peace was never contemplated by the Lord, nor was such an one ever prophesied. But He did bring emancipation to a benighted world, to a people bound in the chains of superstition, lip service, and spiritual bondage. He came and organized His church, set up an eternal program, loosed the bands of death through His own death and resurrection, and outlined and lived before us a perfect plan by which all men might live eternally in joy and peace.

Yes. An individual peace may be had, and certainly millions of individual hearts at peace would go far toward a world at peace. Why should we fight against the tyranny and shackles of nations and at the same time remain in bondage individually to sin? As the world is the sum total of its inhabitants, so also may the world rest and be tranquil if its people are at peace.

Paul taught, "For the kingdom of God is not meat and drink; but righteousness, and peace, and joy in the Holy Ghost. . . . Let us therefore follow after the things which make for peace." (Rom. 14:17, 19.) And Peter added, "For he that will love life, and see good days, let him refrain his tongue from evil, and his lips that they speak no guile: Let him eschew evil, and do good; let him seek peace, and ensue it." (1 Pet. 3:10–11.)

Peace through righteousness; calm assurance through worthiness; a total absence of fear and terror; a tranquility of soul. That is the message of the great Liberator, the Prince of Peace. A personal, individual harmony with our Father in Heaven makes world discord take second place.

35

Can peace be had in the midst of physical torture? The answer comes in the affirmative. I recall a good woman who had been confined in bed for many years—but flat on her back and with a typewriter on her bed, she wrote prose and poetry and brought cheer to many far more fortunate than she was. Joy and happiness she possessed and passed to others.

Another young girl three years paralyzed from an auto accident, unable to move from her bed, was the personification of hope and cheer and peace, and she uplifted all those whose lives she touched. Peace was in her life and she radiated calm and hope.

Lloyd Douglas in his book *The Robe* gave us a sweet picture of a young woman in Palestine, hopelessly paralyzed, whose life was completely changed as it was touched by the Christ's life. Formerly she was morbid, heart-sick, fretful, unreasonable, rebellious. She had resented, these years, her affliction with such self-pity that everyone about her had been miserable. Three years she had lain on her bed, peevish, embittered, refusing to admit even her friends. She had sat smoldering in rebellion. Then came the change. The gospel came into her life, and happiness and contentment reigned therein.

After supper each evening the people of Cana, young and old, assembled at the fountain to hear her sing. They carried her there on a cot. The Savior of the world had walked into her life and a glorious transformation took place. As she sang each day, her face seemed transfigured. There came over her an expression of deep yearning and she seemed to be departing on an enchanted excursion. As she touched the harp strings, her deep contralto voice began softly and swelled steadily into a sweet triumphant song, warm and resonant.

And then someone had asked her, "But why didn't the Christ touch you with the finger of His power and heal you?"

And she answered brightly, "I do not regret my lameness.

Perhaps the people of Cana are more helped by the songs I sing from my cot than they would be if I were physically well. They all have their worries, their agonies, their defeats. If I were whole perhaps they would say: 'Oh! it is easy enough for Miriam to sing and rejoice. She has no trouble. Why shouldn't she sing?' but in my condition, perhaps my songs inspire them, lift them up and give them courage and new strength. Because of my lameness I seem to have very little liberty, but my spirit is free. I enjoy a liberty quite independent of my physical condition. My illness made a wretched slave of me. My peace came as a gift and has liberated me."

Can there be a peace in the midst of disappointment and in persecution, death? A young modern prophet found peace in such a paradoxical situation. The culmination of a long series of bitter persecutions saw this young man in the prime of his life, loving life, enroute to his Golgotha. The Prophet Joseph was approaching Carthage, the place of his massacre, as he well knew. He had been tempted to flee and live, but had met the test, was ready to accept the bitter cup and give his life that his work might live. What a complete surrender of the world! What courage! What peace! No denunciations of his guilty persecutors. No cursing of a treacherous and deadly foe. No bitterness or rage toward his murderers with blackened faces, but a saintly humility and resignation. Without faltering and without hesitation he made his way to his certain death. What courageous endurance! He not only accepted his fate, but seemed to actually confront his tragedy and went out to meet it!

"I am going like a lamb to the slaughter," he said, "but I am calm as a summer's morning; I have a conscience void of offense towards God, and towards all men. I shall die innocent, and it shall yet be said of me—he was murdered in cold blood." (D&C 135:4.)

Here indeed, is the peace that passeth understanding.

37

And then the tranquility in Gethsemane must certainly stir us deeply and convince us that peace comes from within regardless of the clashing scenes without. With perfect knowledge that His hour had come, the Savior knelt alone, unprotected in the garden. He knew well the program, yet loving life He implored the Father, "O my Father, if it be possible, let this cup pass from me: nevertheless not as I will, but as thou wilt" (Matt. 26:39), and after a seemingly interminable period in which his watchers slept, and He suffered untold agonies, and no answer came to His supplications, He prayed again, "O my Father, if this cup may not pass away from me, except I drink it, thy will be done." (Matt. 26:42.)

The armed mob came on with their torches. But no flare of anger came, as Judas, one of His own, betrayed Him with a kiss; no effort to call to His protection the legions of angels which likely stood ready and anxious to deliver Him. His desire was to live, to enjoy His relatives and friends, to teach righteousness to a world so much needing it, to continue a glorious ministry so recently begun. You well know that He did not want to die as you envision Him in His final supplication for a waiver of His martyrdom. But He had volunteered this sacrifice; He had anticipated with reluctance the fulfillment of His own prophecies; He had sweat blood in an incomprehensible suffering and anguish as His hour had come and He met the supreme test and emerged from a catastrophic battle, calm, unruffled, and at peace in a world of clashes, discord, frenzy, hate, and intolerance.

He stood courageously forward, unarmed, in the face of a filthy mob. His murderers fell back, as He demanded, "Be ye come out, as against a thief, with swords and staves?" (Luke 22:52.) No bitterness was in His soul as He bowed to His inevitable duty and as He said calmly to the assassins, "I have told you that I am he: if therefore ye seek me, let these go their way." (John 18:8.) As the fiends fell back, their cowardice and

38

fear was in striking contrast to His courage, His calmness, His strength.

Then again the peace of which He had spoken was shown in its sublimity when He was hanging on the cross in mortal torture. As He thought of His murderers beneath Him, He raised His eyes toward heaven and cried, "Father, forgive them; for they know not what they do." (Luke 23:34.) What character! What peace! Actually blessing them that took His life and shed His blood!

A peace that passeth understanding was the kind enjoyed by the Deacon Stephen. Wrongfully accused, he stood his ground, bore testimony to the truth, and being accused of blasphemy which rated the death penalty, he was taken to the stoning pit for his execution. His assurance of his position with his Maker gave him courage to stand firm. With peace in his soul, he fell to his knees and to the ground as the stones came murderously pounding and torturing his body. His last conscious moments were calm ones. He knew he had lived in harmony with the exalting principles of the gospel of Christ. His dying words were full of forgiveness, "calling upon God, and saying, Lord Jesus, receive my spirit. . . . Lord, lay not this sin to their charge. And when he had said this, he fell asleep." (Acts 7:59–60.)

Again, such tranquility of soul is beautifully portrayed in the large metal monuments in the cemetery at Winter Quarters. Representing the thousands who died between Nauvoo and Salt Lake Valley, this monument depicts a young father and mother standing shoulder to shoulder with bowed heads, their breaking hearts shown in the agony in their faces. As the bitter wintry wind whipped their clothes about them, his right arm held her close; in his hand was the shovel which had so lately completed digging the little open grave in which lay the body of their child. Here was agony, disappointment, loneliness, and sorrow—but not despair. Registered on these sad faces was grim determination, faith, and calm assurance that "God's in His heaven—all's right with the world." And so with the many thousands who crossed the plains. Physical hardship? Yes, with Indians, swollen rivers, blizzards, hunger, and thirst, but within an abiding calm. The things which destroy peace are not famine, pestilence, barbarians, or other external forces, but the obstructing of the channels of communication between one and his God.

"My peace I give unto you" (John 14:27) was the promise of the Savior. What is His peace? And how is it obtained? The answer came clear and unequivocal to the rich young man who asked of the Lord, "Good Master, what good thing shall I do, that I may have eternal life?" The answer: "If thou wilt enter into life, keep the commandments." Because of his extensive possessions with which he was not willing to part, he went away sorrowing. (See Matt. 19:16–22.) He had learned already that peace came not through his wealth or the power and influence of his position. He was told that only perfection of life will bring eternal bliss, and the nearer we all approach perfection, the greater will be our joy and peace.

"For what shall it profit a man, if he shall gain the whole world, and lose his own soul? or what shall a man give in exchange for his soul." (Mark 8:36–37.)

And Paul in his parting thought to the Corinthians said, "Be perfect, be of good comfort, be of one mind, live in peace; and the God of love and peace shall be with you." (2 Cor. 13:11.)

Remember that the peace of God will not come to an unclean person. Only wretchedness and sorrow will be your lot if you follow the call of desire, the spirit of the world. Supply your lamps with oil and keep them burning brightly and follow the path they illuminate. Be ye firm, steadfast, and immovable. Look up with unwavering faith. There is a God whose immutable laws cannot be broken with impunity. Your life will have enough of the disappointments and handicaps without you yourselves adding others. There can come no greater handicap than the loss of faith in God. Permit no one to tear down your faith or to implant within you doubt or question.

Study if you will the philosophies of men, which continue to change, but remember to appraise and evaluate such theories as of human origin. Anchor your faith, your hopes, your future to God who is unchangeable, for He is the same yesterday, today, and forever. If you cannot understand fully today, wait patiently and truth will unfold and light will come. Remember, no one knows all the answers. You do not. Your teachers do not, nor can they. It is as if you are going up the canyon, your vision obscured by the cliffs on either side. Around the jutting hills, across the river, up, up you go, and finally you reach the summit. Your world has suddenly enlarged, bounded now only by the distant mountain ranges of an extended horizon. Over the next range and still new worlds lie ahead to conquer. Be true, patient, trusting. Adjust your philosophy to correspond with the thought of Emerson: "All that I have seen teaches me to trust God for what I have not seen."

Accept unreservedly the fact that God lives, that Jesus is the Christ, that life is eternal, and that the kind of life we live here will determine the degree of eternal joy and peace we shall have throughout that eternity. God will not be mocked.

I say to you with all the sincerity and earnestness I possess, live righteously that your memory will give you roses in December. Live gloriously, as though you would live forever— you will. May the Lord be with you and inspire and guide you as you pursue your duties in a confused world. May you be able, with the clearness of your mind and the strength of your character, to help straighten out the chaos. But may you keep at least your own paths straight and the channel of your communication to your Father in Heaven clear and unblocked, that the static may be eliminated from your life and that your vision may be undimmed as you walk steadily toward the sun-kissed heights on which your ambitious eyes are fixed, and that the peace which passeth understanding may come to you eternally.

———————————————————

President Spencer W. Kimball was ordained an Apostle in 1943, was sustained President of the Church in 1973, and died in 1985. This talk was given in 1944, during World War II.

PART 2

THE PATHWAY TO PEACE

THE PATH TO PEACE

PRESIDENT THOMAS S. MONSON

In all seasons, knowledge of the life and mission of our Lord and Savior, Jesus Christ, comforts our hearts and whispers to our souls the ageless salutation, "Peace be unto you." In a world where peace is such a universal quest, we sometimes wonder why violence walks our streets, accounts of murder and senseless killings fill the columns of our newspapers, and family quarrels and disputes mar the sanctity of the home and smother the tranquility of so many lives.

Perhaps we stray from the path which leads to peace and find it necessary to pause, to ponder, and to reflect on the teachings of the Prince of Peace and determine to incorporate them in our thoughts and actions and to live a higher law, walk a more elevated road, and be a better disciple of Christ.

The ravages of hunger, the brutality of hate, and ethnic struggles across the globe remind us that the peace we seek will not come without effort and determination. Anger, hatred, and contention are foes not easily subdued. These enemies inevitably leave in their destructive wake tears of sorrow, the pain of conflict, and the shattered hopes of what could have been. Their sphere of influence is not restricted to the battlefields of war but can be observed altogether too frequently in the home, around the hearth, and within the heart. So soon do many forget and so late do they remember the counsel of the Lord: "There shall be no disputations among you, . . .

"For verily, verily I say unto you, he that hath the spirit of contention is not of me, but is of the devil, who is the father of contention, and he stirreth up the hearts of men to contend with anger, one with another.

"Behold, this is not my doctrine, to stir up the hearts of men with anger, one against another; but this is my doctrine, that such things should be done away." (3 Ne. 11:28–30.)

As we turn backward the clock of time, we recall that nearly sixty years ago a desperately arranged peace, a conference of peace, convened in the Bavarian city of Munich. Leaders of the European powers assembled even as the world tottered on the brink of war. Their purpose, openly stated, was to pursue a course which they felt would avert war and maintain peace. Mistrust, intrigue, a quest for power doomed to failure that conference. The outcome was not "peace in our time," but rather war and destruction to a degree not previously experienced. Overlooked, or at least set aside, was the hauntingly touching appeal of one who had fallen in an earlier war. He seemed to be writing in behalf of millions of comrades—friend and foe alike:

> In Flanders fields the poppies blow
> Between the crosses, row on row,
> That mark our place; and in the sky
> The larks, still bravely singing, fly
> Scarce heard amid the guns below.
>
> We are the Dead. Short days ago
> We lived, felt dawn, saw sunset glow,
> Loved and were loved, and now we lie
> In Flanders fields.
>
> Take up our quarrel with the foe:
> To you from failing hands we throw
> The torch; be yours to hold it high.

46

If ye break faith with us who die
We shall not sleep, though poppies grow
In Flanders fields.
(John McCrae, "In Flanders Fields," *The
Best Loved Poems of the American People,*
sel. Hazel Felleman [Garden City: Garden
City Publishing Co., 1936], p. 429.)

Are we doomed to repeat the mistakes of the past? After such a brief interval of peace following World War I came the cataclysm of World War II. In 1995 we marked the fiftieth anniversary of the famed landings of Allied forces on the beaches of Normandy. Tens of thousands of dignitaries and veterans flocked to the scene as the landings were reenacted. One writer observed, "Lower Normandy has more than its share of [hallowed dead. Their bodies] lie in graves from Falaise to Cherbourg: 13,796 Americans, 17,958 British, 8,658 Canadian, 650 Polish, and around 65,000 Germans—more than 106,000 dead in all, and that is just the military, all killed in the space of a summer holiday." (David Hewson, *Deseret News,* 13 Mar. 1994, p. T-4.) Similar accounts could be written describing the terrible losses in other theaters of combat in that same conflict.

The famed statesman, William Gladstone, described the formula for peace when he declared: "We look forward to the time when the power of love will replace the love of power. Then will our world know the blessings of peace."

World peace, though a lofty goal, is but an outgrowth of the personal peace each individual seeks to attain. I speak not of the peace promoted by man, but peace as promised of God. I speak of peace in our homes, peace in our hearts, even peace in our lives. Peace after the way of man is perishable. Peace after the manner of God will prevail.

We are reminded that "anger doesn't solve anything. It builds nothing, but it can destroy everything." (L. Douglas

Wilder, *Deseret News,* 1 Dec. 1991, p. A-2.) The consequences of conflict are so devastating that we yearn for guidance—even a way to insure our success as we seek the path to peace. What is the way to obtain such a universal blessing? Are there prerequisites? Let us remember that to obtain God's blessings, one must do God's bidding. May I suggest three ideas to prompt our thinking and guide our footsteps: 1. Search inward; 2. Reach outward; and 3. Look heavenward.

First: Search inward. Self-evaluation is always a difficult procedure. We are so frequently tempted to gloss over areas which demand correction and dwell endlessly on our individual strengths. President Ezra Taft Benson counseled us: "The price of peace is righteousness. Men and nations may loudly proclaim, 'Peace, peace,' but there shall be no peace until individuals nurture in their souls those principles of personal purity, integrity, and character which foster the development of peace. Peace cannot be imposed. It must come from the lives and hearts of men. There is no other way." ("Purposeful Living," *Listen, A Journal of Better Living,* Jan.-Mar. 1955, p. 19.)

Elder Richard L. Evans observed: "To find peace—the peace within, the peace that passeth understanding—men must live in honesty, honoring each other, honoring obligations, working willingly, loving and cherishing loved ones, serving and considering others, with patience, with virtue, with faith and forbearance, with the assurance that life is for learning, for serving, for repenting, and improving. And God be thanked for the blessed principle of repenting and improving, which is a way that is open to us all." (Conference Report, Oct. 1959, p. 128.)

The place of parents in the home and family is of vital importance as we examine our personal responsibilities in this regard. Recently, a distinguished group met in conference to examine the increase of violence in the lives of individuals, particularly the young. Some observations from their deliberations are helpful to us as we examine our priorities: "A society that views graphic violence as entertainment . . . should not be surprised when senseless violence shatters the dreams of its youngest and brightest. . . .

"Unemployment and despair can lead to desperation. But most people will not commit desperate acts if they have been taught that dignity, honesty and integrity are more important than revenge or rage; if they understand that respect and kindness ultimately give one a better chance at success. . . .

"The women of the anti-violence summit have hit on the solution—the only one that can reverse a downward spiral of destructive behavior and senseless pain. A return to old-fashioned family values will work wonders." (*Deseret News,* 16 Jan. 1994, p. A-12.)

So frequently we mistakenly believe that our children need more things, when in reality their silent pleadings are simply for more of our time. The accumulation of wealth or the multiplication of assets belie the Master's teaching: "Lay not up for yourselves treasures upon earth, where moth and rust doth corrupt, and where thieves break through and steal: But lay up for yourselves treasures in heaven, where neither moth nor rust doth corrupt, and where thieves do not break through nor steal. For where your treasure is, there will your heart be also."(Matt. 6:19–21.)

One evening I saw large masses of parents and children crossing an intersection in Salt Lake City en route to the Delta Center to see the Disney on Ice production of *Beauty and the Beast.* I actually pulled my car over to the curb to watch the gleeful throng. Fathers, who I am certain were cajoled into going to the event, held tightly in their hands the small and clutching hands of their precious children. Here was love in action. Here was an unspoken sermon of caring. Here was a rearranging of time as a God-given priority.

49

Truly peace will reign triumphant when we improve ourselves after the pattern taught by the Lord. Then we will appreciate the deep spirituality hidden behind the simple words of a familiar song: "There is beauty all around when there's love at home." (*Hymns*, 1985, no. 294.)

Second: Reach outward. Though exaltation is a personal matter, and while individuals are saved not as a group but indeed as individuals, yet one cannot live in a vacuum. Membership in the Church calls forth a determination to serve. A position of responsibility may not be of recognized importance, nor may the reward be broadly known. Service, to be acceptable to the Savior, must come from willing minds, ready hands, and pledged hearts.

Occasionally discouragement may darken our pathway; frustration may be a constant companion. In our ears there may sound the sophistry of Satan as he whispers, "You cannot save the world; your small efforts are meaningless. You haven't time to be concerned for others." Trusting in the Lord, let us turn our heads from such falsehoods and make certain our feet are firmly planted in the path of service and our hearts and souls dedicated to follow the example of the Lord. In moments when the light of resolution dims and when the heart grows faint, we can take comfort from His promise: "Be not weary in well-doing. . . . Out of small things proceedeth that which is great. Behold, the Lord requireth the heart and a willing mind." (D&C 64:33–34.)

In 1993, the Primary organization conducted an effort to have the children become better acquainted with the holy temples of God. Frequently this entailed a visit to the temple grounds. The laughter of small children, the joy of unfettered youth, and the exuberance of energy displayed by them gladdened the heart of this observer. As a loving teacher guided a boy or girl to the large door of the Salt Lake Temple and the little one reached out and up to touch the temple, I could almost see the Master welcoming the little children to His side and could almost hear His comforting words: "Suffer the little children to come unto me, and forbid them not: for of such is the kingdom of God." (Mark 10:14.)

Number three: Look heavenward. As we do, we find it comforting and satisfying to communicate with our Heavenly Father through prayer, that path to spiritual power—even a passport to peace. We are reminded of His beloved Son, the Prince of Peace, that pioneer who literally showed the way for others to follow. His divine plan can save us from the Babylons of sin, complacency, and error. His example points the way. When faced with temptation, He shunned it. When offered the world, He declined it. When asked for His life, He gave it.

On one significant occasion, Jesus took a text from Isaiah: "The Spirit of the Lord God is upon me; because the Lord hath anointed me to preach good tidings unto the meek; he hath sent me to bind up the brokenhearted, to proclaim liberty to the captives, and the opening of the prison to them that are bound" (Isa. 61:1)—a clear pronouncement of the peace that passeth all understanding.

Frequently, death comes as an intruder. It is an enemy that suddenly appears in the midst of life's feast, putting out its lights and its gaiety. Death lays its heavy hand upon those dear to us and, at times, leaves us baffled and wondering. In certain situations, as in great suffering and illness, death comes as an angel of mercy. But to those bereaved, the Master's promise of peace is the comforting balm which heals: "Peace I leave with you, my peace I give unto you: not as the world giveth, give I unto you. Let not your heart be troubled, neither let it be afraid." (John 14:27.) "I go to prepare a place for you . . . ; that where I am, there ye may be also." (John 14:2–3.)

How I pray that all who have loved then lost might know the reality of the resurrection and have the unshakable knowledge that families can be forever. One such was a Major Sullivan Ballou, who, during the time of the American Civil War, wrote a touching letter to his wife—just one week before he was killed in the Battle of Bull Run. With me, feel the love of his soul, his trust in God, his courage, his faith.

July 14, 1861, Camp Clark, Washington

My very dear Sarah,

The indications are very strong that we shall move in a few days—perhaps tomorrow. Lest I should not be able to write again, I feel impelled to write a few lines that may fall under your eye when I shall be no more.

I have no misgivings about, or lack of confidence in, the cause in which I am engaged, and my courage does not halt or falter. . . . I am . . . perfectly willing . . . to lay down all my joys in this life, to help maintain this Government. . . .

Sarah, my love for you is deathless; it seems to bind me with mighty cables that nothing but Omnipotence could break; and yet my love of Country comes over me like a strong wind and bears me unresistably on with all these chains to the battle field.

The memories of the blissful moments I have spent with you come creeping over me, and I feel most gratified to God and to you that I have enjoyed them so long. And hard it is for me to give them up and burn to ashes the hopes of future years, when, God willing, we might still have lived and loved together, and seen our sons grown up to honorable manhood around us. I have, I know, but few and small claims upon Divine Providence, but something whispers to me—perhaps it is the wafted prayer of my little Edgar, that I shall return to my loved ones unharmed. If I do not, my dear Sarah, never forget how much I love you, and when my last breath escapes me on the battle field, it will whisper your name. Forgive [me] my . . . faults, and the many pains I have caused you. How thoughtless and foolish I have oftentimes been! How gladly would I wash out with my tears every little spot upon your happiness. . . .

But, O Sarah! If the dead can come back to this earth and the unseen around those they loved, I shall always be near you; in the gladdest days and in the darkest nights . . . always, always, and if there be a soft breeze upon your cheek, it shall be my breath; as the cool air fans your throbbing temple, it shall be my spirit passing by. Sarah, do not mourn me dead; think I am gone and wait for thee, for we shall meet again. (Dennis Lythgoe, *Deseret News,* 16 Oct. 1990, p. C-3.)

The darkness of death can ever be dispelled by the light of revealed truth. "I am the resurrection, and the life," spoke the Master. "He that believeth in me, though he were dead, yet shall he live: And whosoever liveth and believeth in me shall never die." (John 11:25–26.) Added to His own words are those of the angel, spoken to the weeping Mary Magdalene and the other Mary as they approached the tomb to care for the body of their Lord: "Why seek ye the living among the dead? He is not here, but is risen." (Luke 24:5–6.)

Such is the message of the gospel of Jesus Christ. He lives! And because He lives all shall indeed live again. This knowledge provides the peace for loved ones of those whose graves are marked by the crosses of Normandy, those hallowed resting places in Flanders fields where the poppies blow in springtime, and for those who rest in countless other locations, including the depths of the sea. "Oh, sweet the joy this sentence gives: 'I know that my Redeemer lives!'" (*Hymns,* 1985, no. 136.)

President Thomas S. Monson was ordained an Apostle in 1963. He was called to serve in the First Presidency of the Church in 1985.

THE NATURE OF PEACE

ELDER JOHN A. WIDTSOE

This is a Church of peace. The gospel of the Lord Jesus Christ is a gospel of peace. The head of the Church, the Lord Jesus Christ, is the Prince of Peace. If we study the conditions of the Church, its principles, its practices, all that pertains to it, we shall find that they all converge upon one great objective—the establishment of peace upon earth and among the children of men. That is the objective which dates back to the beginning of mortal time.

This matter of peace appears and reappears in the scriptures. As the Savior said: "Peace I leave with you, my peace I give unto you." (John 14:27.)

At this particular time in the world's history, we have much to say about peace. The devil for some time has been given ample dominion over his own; but we understand that there never was a time when the hand of the Lord was wholly withdrawn from human affairs. Apparently the tide of battle is now being turned by the Lord toward victory for those who are battling for righteous principles.

Therefore, men are speaking about peace and what is going to happen after the [Second World War]. Books and articles are being published, there is a deluge of written material setting up propositions and proposals relative to the disposition of all mankind and all human affairs after the war is over.

These proposals begin at the wrong end, and they will all fail. Peace upon earth is not to be established by Congress or Parliament or by a group of international representatives. Peace is not a thing that can be taken on, then taken off again, as we do a piece of clothing. Peace is quite different from that. Peace cannot be legislated into existence. It is not the way to lasting peace upon earth.

Remember, the Savior himself tried to point that out to us, for when he spoke to his disciples and said, "Peace I leave with you, my peace I give unto you," he added, "Not as the world giveth, give I unto you." (John 14:27.)

Peace comes from within; peace is myself, if I am a truly peaceful man. The very essence of me must be the spirit of peace. Individuals make up the community, and the nation—an old enough doctrine, which we often overlook—and the only way to build a peaceful community is to build men and women who are lovers and makers of peace. Each individual, by that doctrine of Christ and his Church, holds in his own hands the peace of the world.

That makes me responsible for the peace of the world, and makes you individually responsible for the peace of the world. The responsibility cannot be shifted to someone else. It cannot be placed upon the shoulders of Congress or Parliament, or any other organization of men with governing authority.

I wonder if the Lord did not have that in mind when he said: "The kingdom of God is within you" (Luke 17:21), or perhaps we should reemphasize it and say: "The kingdom of God is within *you*."

I believe that our problems in this day and age are in some respects the most terrible in the whole history of the world, and the most difficult to understand. Yet we know that peace and all that pertains to it must come from within honest human hearts who have been drilled and tested in righteousness.

The question may be asked, Is it really possible for such individuals to be vanquished, shall we say, by peace? Is it possible for such individuals to be so multiplied in number, as to make of the earth a happy, peaceful dwelling place. The answer which we give to the world is that if a man but conform to, if he be in harmony with, eternal law, peace will be his. That is a simple formula which refers to body, mind, and spirit, and to our neighbors. If I obey the physical laws of the body, physical peace will be mine. If I obey the laws of mental health, I shall be mentally at peace. If I obey the spiritual laws which God has given, I shall likewise find peace, the highest peace. If I love my neighbors, even as I love myself and my God, and all men do the same, there will be complete social peace. Such obedience can be yielded; such harmony can be won. It has been done by men; it can be done again. Such harmony with law lies at the foundation of the problem of our searching and reaching out for peace in our troubled world.

There may be some who have tried to pay only a part of the tithing due the Lord. Has peace remained in their hearts? Ask ourselves! There may be those who have been taught the Word of Wisdom, and have failed to keep it. There is not peace in our hearts when we disobey the law. Conformity to the law alone brings peace.

But before we can obey we must know and understand the law. Thereby hangs a tale so long that it is impossible to discuss it in these few pages. Peace has been lost because the world has lost the knowledge of divine truth, or knowing it, has misunderstood it.

For example, God, who needs to be known first, has been made into an ethereal essence, filling space, which, as the Father of men, is incomprehensible to the human mind. It is folly to look for peace among men when the deeper realities of existence are not understood. Men are ill at ease who do not comprehend these truths correctly, and are prone to warfare. Only as the truths of existence are found and accepted will peace prevail on earth.

Men must also understand the plan of salvation, the meaning of life, to find peace in their own hearts, and to help establish peace on earth. I remember the hostile British officer who attempted to prevent my entrance into Great Britain because I was a "Mormon." In the ensuing conversation he said finally: "If I admit you, what will you do in Great Britain?"

I answered: "If you admit me, I shall, to the best of my ability teach the people of Great Britain how to win happiness in this life and the life hereafter. I shall tell them whence they came, why they are here upon this earth, and where they are going after death."

The uniformed man, a long-time servant of the empire, looked at me in astonishment. "Can you answer these questions? All my life I have sought answers to them. No one has been able to answer me. Please teach me."

He was not at peace; he was uneasy in his heart.

I remember the aged widow in southern Utah, a convert from England, who had left a cultured home to begin the pioneer toil of building an empire here in the western desert. She told of her struggles and sacrifices, of the pains of her days and years. When she had told the story, one to bring tears to my eyes, I said to her, "Sister, yours has been a hard life; you have sacrificed much. Let me ask you, if you were a girl again in England and could look down the coming years, would you do it again? Would you accept the gospel and face the life that you have here lived?"

The old lady, in her eighties, got up from her chair, looked me in the eye: "You ask me, would I do it again? For that which the gospel has given me, I would do it over again ten thousand times." She had found peace. Her heart was at ease.

There is no time to discuss further the method by which individual peace may be won, but it may be added that the seeker after peace must forget himself in the search. The art of placing the cause above oneself is of first importance if peace shall grow in our hearts. Whenever we place ourselves before the cause, we are, in the words of President John Taylor, in the hands of evil. The peace disappears.

Let me add one thing more. There is a statement in the Doctrine and Covenants which I have read with many a sober thought:

"Every man that will not take his sword against his neighbor must needs flee unto Zion for safety. And there shall be gathered unto it out of every nation under heaven; and it shall be the only people that shall not be at war one with another." (D&C 45:68–69.)

They shall "flee unto Zion for safety." That I believe does not mean a geographically limited place, but a place where the pure in heart dwell, for they are Zion, and out of that Zion consisting of the pure in heart shall go forth the force and power that will bring peace to pass upon this unhappy earth.

We are Zion; we say we are; I know we are. We are under the tremendous commission so to live, so to establish peace in our own hearts as to make our companionship, wherever we are, a society to which the suffering, the uneasy, those without peace, in all the world, may flee for safety. Truly a tremendous obligation rests upon the Latter-day Saints.

We have been taught that this people is a leaven. We know that to be true. We are as a leaven to all the world. Thus, future, lasting peace is not a question of majority or minority, but of the power of the leaven. The leaven may be weak. Sometimes it needs to be strengthened. That is our problem, especially the task of leadership, to strengthen among our people the leaven of peace, the gospel of peace, so that out of our very presence, out of our hearts and faith, something radiates that will touch the hearts of all who are seekers after truth, who are lovers of peace. As such people gather to us, if we do our duty, they will be blessed and find that which they seek, and with us help establish upon earth the kingdom of peace, which is the kingdom of heaven.

"Blessed are the peacemakers: for they shall be called the children of God." (Matt. 5:9.)

My message to you, and my plea with you is that each one of us, in behalf of himself, his flock, the world, will constitute himself a peacemaker, beginning with his own heart, to cleanse it, to make it fit for the abode of peace.

Elder John A. Widtsoe was ordained an Apostle in 1921; he died in 1952.

THE PEACE THAT COMES THROUGH RIGHTEOUSNESS

PRESIDENT HENRY D. MOYLE

There is one thing in the world today above all else which people are seeking after, and that is peace.

The fundamental purpose of the organization of the Church is to establish peace upon the earth.

President David O. McKay taught that "peace is the exemption from individual troubles, from family brawls, from national difficulties. Peace does not come to the transgressor of law. Peace comes by obedience to law—peace to the individual that he may be at peace with God, at peace in the home, and in the neighborhood. The spirit of the world is antagonistic to the establishment of peace. The law of nature seems to be the survival of the fittest at all costs. But peace can come into the world only through obedience to the gospel of Jesus Christ." Seek first the kingdom of God and his righteousness. Jesus' teaching regarding arbitration as a means of settling difficulties, if applied by nations, would do away with war.

"The gospel is a complete way of life, and the true plan of life brings joy and peace," said President McKay. Fundamental to the doctrines of the Church is the declaration of Father Lehi:

"Adam fell that men might be; and men are, that they might have joy." (2 Ne. 2:25.)

The teachings of our President are not the development of a philosophy by the wisdom of men that changes with time and experience. They do not result from the trial and error of improvement. They are not discovered as the result of laboratory experiments on the one hand or study of the past, present, or future on the other hand. They are eternal truths taught to the children of men by the prophets of God, ancient and modern. The truths of the gospel are unchangeable. They are infallible. The Savior of mankind—our Redeemer, the Son of the living God, the Lord of lords and King of kings, who rules and reigns over this universe, brought peace to this earth as he dwelt among the children of men in the flesh. He is the man of peace. He came with a promise: "Blessed are the peacemakers: for they shall be called the children of God." (Matt. 5:9.)

Except with peace in our hearts we cannot be the children of God. This follows just as certainly as do all the promises given us by our Master in his Sermon on the Mount. Surely we cannot expect to see God if we are not pure in heart. We bear witness to the world by virtue of the power and authority of the holy priesthood of God which we bear that the words of his mouth contained in the sacred Beatitudes were not platitudes or trite sayings to catch the ear of man, spoken by a humanitarian, but on the contrary, they are the words of God spoken by his Son Jesus Christ, upon which all the children of men can place their trust unfalteringly and conform their lives, their thoughts and actions, to merit in this life and in the life to come all the blessings promised those who are faithful and obedient to his teachings—not only the Sermon on the Mount, but all that he taught during his ministry here upon this earth as he sojourned among men, and all that he has revealed to his prophets to the present time.

John, in his Gospel, says: "These things I have spoken unto you," quoting the Savior, "that in me ye might have peace. In the world ye shall have tribulation: but be of good cheer; I have overcome the world." (John 16:33.)

Paul said: "Let the peace of God rule in your hearts." (Col. 3:15.)

Unfortunately, many in the world, both individuals and nations, will ignore the teachings of Christ and deny his divinity. With two powers upon earth exerting their influence upon mankind this result is inevitable. They, through their own conduct, their own choice, do not qualify for the enjoyment of peace, and peace will not be theirs. The history of the world has already altogether too clearly demonstrated that the farther we depart from the gospel of Jesus Christ, the greater is the distress and tribulation under which we live.

Should those who keep the commandments of God have any fear for their own security and happiness? This is an interesting question, and this again has been answered so often in the ministry of President David O. McKay. He assures us that we need have no worry. We will never be left in the dark, and we should have no concern other than to follow the leadership God has given us here upon the earth.

We are the children of promise as long as we keep the commandments of God. I have no doubt it will take continuous effort, however, upon our part. These are not blessings which will flow to us automatically merely because we ask for them. We will be justified, however, if we follow all that God reveals through his servants, the prophets. We have been given direction, sometimes thought of as temporal in its nature, such as tithing, fast offerings, the welfare program, the Word of Wisdom, chastity, obedience to the law of the land, and others. Whatever their temporal aspect may be, they are given to us to build us up spiritually. We can draw no hard and fast line between temporal and spiritual. All that is good is spiritual.

So we can well afford to ask ourselves the question: Can we

expect the blessings of peace if we ignore the Word of Wisdom, for example? Will we be prepared to take advantage of the ways and means our Father in heaven may make available for us to retain our peace in times of great emergency, indeed at all times, if we are not physically fit? I have no doubt God will require us to be sound in mind and body to carry on the work of his priesthood at home and abroad, at least as far as we by our own efforts can retain our bodily and spiritual health and strength. We cannot be justified in destroying ourselves through our disobedience, no matter how limited our conduct in this direction may be.

It is an inspiration to me, and I hope it will be to you, to reflect for a moment upon the teachings we have received through our inspired prophets in these latter days. Though times have changed, and conditions in the world are different, neither the hearts of men nor the revelations of God to his people through his prophets have changed. We read in the Holy Bible: "Surely the Lord God will do nothing, but he revealeth his secret unto his servants the prophets." (Amos 3:7.)

I know by the testimony of the Holy Ghost that is in me that this declaration of Amos is literally true in the ministry of our present prophet as it was in the life of Joseph Smith and those who followed the first Prophet in these latter days in this high and holy office. "It is out of the abundance of the heart that man speaketh," said Joseph Smith, "and the man who tells you words of life is the man who can save you." (See *Times and Seasons* 5:616.)

What Joseph Smith said in 1844 in principle is largely applicable today, although our problems are somewhat different and the remedy prescribed unique to the solution of the specific problem that then confronted the nation. The nation did not accept his solution, which was inspired of God. Had his direction been given to the problem, we all know what the result would have been—no bloodshed. Both the Civil War and its aftermath, with us even now, and the economic loss of both would have been avoided. What happened to those who followed his leadership and direction? Even though the Prophet Joseph was martyred, two months after this solution to our national ills was publicly given, the Saints were driven from their peaceful homes in the states to a haven of safety in the fastness of this mountain region. That is where they were when the Civil War began.

Certainly God works in a mysterious way, his wonders to perform. Who would have ever thought among the inhabitants of Nauvoo in the days of the final persecution that they were being driven from their homes by their enemies against their will and against their better judgment, only to wake up one day and find that the Lord had preserved them in a land of peace, even in the midst of the greatest of all civil wars. Who doubts that the Lord can do what he pleases with his people today?

I have implicit faith in the words of the prophet when he tells us today that all we need to worry about is to keep the commandments of God, and peace will be ours. We do not know when or where or what exactly may happen. It is therefore foolish and impossible to conjecture on the nature of the relief or protection or security designed for the future accomplishment of God's purpose.

This, however, we do know: that God lives and in him we can trust, and through our obedience we are now free from fear or doubt or insecurity, and shall remain so always, as long as we retain the right through our faithfulness to call upon him for the blessings which he has promised the faithful.

I conceive of peace as something which we might all enjoy, even in the midst of future wars. We may suffer trials and tribulations. We may suffer from the loss of our loved ones, but let us stop for a moment and call just two instances to mind. I think of the Prophet Joseph that night after he had left Nauvoo with some of his close brethren and crossed over to the other side of the river to Montrose, and there the question was, should he go on, or should he go back? It was during these days that the Prophet said that he was devoid of offense toward any man, and that he would be taken as a lamb to the slaughter, but does anybody have any doubt in his mind but that the peace of God was in his heart and in his soul and gave him the strength and the courage and the power of his priesthood to fulfil his mission here upon the earth as God might decree?

The other great example, of course, supersedes all else in human knowledge and understanding, and that is the intercessory prayer of the Lord and Savior Jesus Christ as he prayed to his Father in heaven in the Garden of Gethsemane. But there was peace in his heart when he said, "Nevertheless, Father, thy will, not mine, be done." (See Luke 22:42.)

Now that peace can come into our hearts, no matter what the circumstances may be, and no matter what process or what circumstance the Lord may use to bring his faithful people the peace which he has promised them. I have an abiding conviction that if that peace is given to us and we are called upon to lose our lives or the lives of our loved ones, that we will have the absolute assurance, as did the Prophet Joseph, that we would die in the Lord, and when we die in the Lord we have fulfilled the will of the Master here upon this earth, to his pleasure and to his satisfaction, and more can be gained by none of us.

No greater power can exist upon the earth than the power of the priesthood—a gift of God to us—calling upon us to exercise our power as elders in Israel to bring all nations which permit us within their borders to a knowledge of the truth; to draw out those nations, not necessarily physically, but into these stakes of Zion which are being and will continue to be organized in the various countries of the world. These men and women through

66

their faith, conversion, and their faithfulness will join with us as recipients of these greatest of all blessings which the Lord has in store for his chosen people. So, neither they nor we need to worry about our security when we know that our welfare will be taken care of directly from the throne of God on High.

I first quoted from President David O. McKay's teachings, and now I want to quote just a word or two from the other Presidents of the Church to show how uniformly the Lord has revealed his will to his prophets in these latter days.

Joseph Smith said: "Make honor the standard with all men. Be sure that good is rendered for evil in all cases; and the whole nation, like a kingdom of kings and priests, will rise up in righteousness, and be respected as wise and worthy on earth, and as just and holy for heaven, by Jehovah, the Author of perfection." (*Times and Seasons* 5:532.)

Brigham Young said: "Great peace have they who love the law of the Lord and abide in his commandments. Our belief will bring peace to all men and good will to all the inhabitants of the earth. It will induce all who sincerely follow its dictates to cultivate righteousness and peace; to live peaceably in their families; to praise the Lord morning and evening; to pray with their families, and will so fill them with the spirit of peace that they will never condemn or chasten any one unless it is well deserved." (*Discourses of Brigham Young,* sel. John A. Widtsoe [Salt Lake City: Deseret Book Co., 1941], pp. 223, 449.)

It is interesting to see what John Taylor in his day said: "This peace is the gift of God alone, and it can be received only from him by obedience to his laws. If any man wishes to introduce peace into his family or among his friends, let him cultivate it in his own bosom; for sterling peace can only be had according to the legitimate rule and authority of heaven and obedience to its laws." (*The Gospel Kingdom,* comp. G. Homer Durham [Salt Lake City: Bookcraft, 1943], p. 319.)

Wilford Woodruff said: "Put your trust in God and rely on his promises, living up to the light and knowledge you possess; and all will be well with you whether living or dying." (*Discourses of Wilford Woodruff,* sel. G. Homer Durham [Salt Lake City: Bookcraft, 1946], p. 260.)

President Lorenzo Snow, from a document published in the *Deseret News* of January 1, 1901, said:

"A new century dawns upon the world today. The hundred years just completed were the most momentous in the history of man upon this planet. It would be impossible to make even a brief summary of the notable events, the marvelous developments, the grand achievements, and the beneficial inventions and discoveries, which mark the progress of ten decades now left behind in the ceaseless march of humanity. The very mention of the nineteenth century suggests advancement, improvement, liberty, and light. Happy are we to have lived amidst its wonders and shared in the richness of its treasures of intelligence.

"The lessons of the past century should have prepared us for the duties and glories of the opening era. It ought to be the age of peace, of greater progress, of the universal adoption of the golden rule. Barbarism of the past should be buried. War with its horrors should be but a memory. The aim of nations should be fraternity and mutual greatness. The welfare of humanity should be studied instead of the enrichment of a race or the extension of an empire. Awake, ye monarchs of the earth and rulers among nations and gaze upon the scene on which the early rays of the rising millennial day gild the morning of the twentieth century!

"The power is in your hands to pave the way for the coming of the King of kings, whose dominion will be over all the earth. Disband your armies; turn your weapons of strife into implements of industry; take the yoke from the necks of the people; arbitrate your disputes; meet in royal congress and plan for union instead of conquest, for the banishment of poverty, for the uplifting of the masses, and for the health, wealth, enlightenment, and happiness of all tribes and peoples and nations. Then shall the twentieth century be to you the glory of your lives and the lustre of your crowns, and posterity will sing your praises, while the Eternal One shall place you on high among the mighty. . . .

"In the eighty-seventh year of my age on earth, I am full of earnest desire for the benefit of humanity. I wish all a Happy New Year. . . . May justice triumph and corruption be stamped out. And may virtue, chastity, and honor prevail, until evil shall be overcome and the earth shall be cleansed from wickedness. Let these sentiments, as the voice of the 'Mormons' in the mountains of Utah, go forth to the whole world, and let all people know that our wish and our mission are for the blessing and salvation of the entire human race.

"May the twentieth century prove the happiest, as it will be the grandest, for all the ages of time, and may God be glorified in the victory that is coming over sin, sorrow, misery, and death. Peace be unto you all."

Joseph F. Smith said: "There is only one thing that can bring peace into the world. It is the adoption of the gospel of Jesus Christ, rightly understood, obeyed and practiced by rulers and people alike." (*Gospel Doctrine* [Salt Lake City: Deseret Book Co., 1928], p. 529.) I love such words of scripture.

And President Grant said: "This gospel of Jesus Christ which the world says is a delusion, a snare, and a fraud, [yet] to each and every man who goes out to proclaim it, and who lives an upright and virtuous life, it brings peace, it brings joy, it brings happiness unspeakable." (Conference Report, October 1911, p. 22.)

At the October conference of 1921 President Grant presented a "Peace Resolution," representing the Church as favoring world peace, and invoking blessings and "divine guidance of the International Conference of the Limitations of Armaments, that the cause of Peace may be thereby enhanced, and an amelioration of the burdens of mankind secured." (Conference Report, October 1921, p. 192.)

President George Albert Smith once prayed: "And, O Father, in the midst of confusion that is everywhere, and uncertainty, bless us in America, that we may repent of our foolishness, our light-mindedness and our wrongdoing, realizing as we should, that all the blessings that are worthwhile come to us only as a result of honoring thee and keeping thy commandments. The pathway of righteousness is the highway of peace and happiness." (*Church News*, Aug. 2, 1947.)

And then finally, to end, I come back to where I began, to the words of President McKay: "The Need of Peace: The greatest need of this old world today is peace. The turbulent storms of hate, enmity, of distrust, and of sin are threatening to wreck humanity. It is time for men—true men—to dedicate their lives to God, and to cry with the spirit and power of the Christ, 'Peace, be still.' Only in the complete surrender of our inner life may we rise above the selfish, sordid pull of nature. We should seek first the kingdom of God and his righteousness. What the spirit is to the body, God is to the spirit. As the body dies when the spirit leaves it, so the spirit dies when we exclude God from it. I cannot imagine peace in a world from which God and religion are banished." (*Millennial Star* 85:802.)

President Henry D. Moyle was ordained an Apostle in 1947, was called into the First Presidency of the Church in 1959, and died in 1963.

PEACE THROUGH PRAYER

ELDER REX D. PINEGAR

I would like to offer my testimony of the blessing of peace that comes through the miraculous power of prayer.

Alexandre Dumas, in his classic tale *The Count of Monte Cristo,* wrote, "For the happy man prayer is only a jumble of words, until the day when sorrow comes to explain to him the sublime language by means of which he speaks to God." (Trans. Lowell Bair [New York: Bantam Books, 1981], p. 34.)

It was a happy, carefree time in my young life until on such a day, sorrow and tragedy brought me closer to God in humble, sincere prayer. In the summer of my thirteenth year, on a July night, I eagerly joined some neighborhood friends to light fireworks. Five of us took turns igniting the colorful assortment of Roman candles and rockets and firecrackers. Each was a new surprise with its burst of sights and sounds through the evening sky.

Not all of our fireworks worked as they should have. Most, in fact, were what we called duds. They sputtered momentarily, and then died. We set the duds aside until we had tried to light all of the fireworks. We had so many defective ones remaining, we wondered what to do. We couldn't just throw them away. What if we emptied the powder from all of them into the cardboard box? We could toss in a match and have one gigantic blast!

71

Fortunately for us, our idea failed—at first. The match was tossed; we quickly ran away and waited. Nothing happened. Pressing our luck, we tried a second time, using a makeshift fuse of rolled-up newspaper. Again we anxiously waited at a distance. Again, to our good, nothing happened. That is when we should have quit. Foolishly, we gave it one more try; this time my friend Mark and I huddled around the box to keep the flame from being extinguished by the evening breeze.

Then it happened! The "gigantic blast" we thought we wanted exploded with fury into our faces. The force of the explosion knocked us off our feet, and flames from the ignited powder burned us severely. It was a tragic scene. Responding quickly to the screams and cries of the injured youth in her driveway, our friend's mother gathered us into her home. "First we will pray," she said, "and then we will call the doctor." That was the first of many prayers I remember being offered for us.

Soon after, I felt my face, hands, and arms being wrapped in bandages. I heard the voices of my father and my doctor administering a priesthood blessing to me. I heard my mother's voice many times, pleading with Heavenly Father to please let her son see again.

I had been taught very early in my life to pray. Mother and Father had made prayer an important part of our family life. Not until that day, however, did it become so meaningful to me. In those frightening moments I found peace and comfort through prayer.

Recently in his own pain and suffering, my friend and associate Elder Clinton Cutler said of his experience, "The Lord's peace comes not without pain, but in the midst of pain."

Our Father in Heaven has promised us peace in times of trial and has provided a way for us to come to Him in our need. He has given us the privilege and power of prayer. He has told us to "pray always" and has promised He will pour out His Spirit upon us. (D&C 19:38.)

Thankfully, we can call upon Him anytime, anywhere. We can speak to Him in the quiet thoughts of our mind and from the deepest feelings of our heart. It has been said, "Prayer is made up of heart throbs and the righteous yearnings of the soul." (James E. Talmage, *Jesus the Christ* [Salt Lake City: Deseret Book Co., 1977], p. 238.) Our Heavenly Father has told us He knows our thoughts and the intents of our heart. (See D&C 6:16.)

President Marion G. Romney taught, "Sometimes the Lord puts thoughts in our minds in answer to prayers. . . . [He] gives us peace in our minds." (Taiwan Area Conference, 1975, p. 7.)

For example, in response to Oliver Cowdery's prayer to know if the translation of the plates by Joseph Smith was true, the Lord answered, "Did I not speak peace to your mind concerning the matter? What greater witness can you have than from God?" (D&C 6:23.)

The peace God speaks to our minds will let us know when decisions we have made are right, when our course is true. It can come as personal inspiration and guidance to assist us in our daily life—in our homes, in our work. It can provide us with courage and hope to meet the challenges of life. The miracle of prayer, to me, is that in the private, quiet chambers of our mind and heart, God both hears *and* answers prayers.

Perhaps the greatest test of our faith and the most difficult part of prayer may be to recognize the answer that comes to us in a thought or a feeling, and then to accept or to act upon the answer God chooses to give. Consistency in prayer, along with searching the scriptures and following the counsel of living prophets, keeps us in tune with the Lord and enables us to interpret the promptings of the Spirit more easily. The Lord has said:

73

"Learn of me, and listen to my words; walk in the meekness of my Spirit, and you shall have peace in me." (D&C 19:23.)

Some time ago I attended the funeral of a lifelong friend, Ralph Poulsen. He was a righteous man of accomplishment and integrity, yet he had to endure the pain and sorrow inflicted upon him by the consequences of a cruel disease. His dear wife, Joyce, suffered also as she was by his side through his agony and pain. As the days and years of suffering went on, she arrived at a time when she felt she could not handle another day. She had done all she could for him. Now a strength beyond her own was needed. In the depth of her sorrow, she pleaded more fervently to God for His help. With the morning came a blessed peace that filled her whole soul—a peace that has continued with her to this day.

There *is* terrible suffering in our world today. Tragic things happen to good people. God does not cause them, nor does He always prevent them. He does, however, strengthen us and bless us with His peace, through earnest prayer.

"It is not the usual purpose of prayer to serve us like Aladdin's lamp, to bring us ease without effort," Elder Richard L. Evans wrote. "Prayer is not a matter of asking only. It should not be always as the beggar's upturned hand. Often the purpose of prayer is to give us strength to do what needs to be done, wisdom to see the way to solve our own problems, and ability to do our best in our tasks.

"We need to pray . . . for strength to endure, for faith and fortitude to face what sometimes must be faced." (*The Man and the Message* [Salt Lake City: Bookcraft, 1973], p. 289.)

It was the Lord Himself who taught us by His own example how to find peace when the answers we receive are not what we asked for. On the eve of His crucifixion, with "soul . . . exceeding sorrowful, even unto death," Jesus knelt in the Garden of Gethsemane and prayed to the Father, saying, "O my Father, if it be possible [and he acknowledged 'all things are possible unto thee'], let this cup pass from me: nevertheless not as I will, but as thou wilt." (Matt. 26:38–39; see also Mark 14:36.)

We can only try to imagine the anguish the Savior felt when we read in the Gospels that He was "sore amazed, and . . . very heavy" (Mark 14:33), that He "fell on his face" and prayed not once, but a second time, and then a third (Matt. 26:39, 42, 44). "Father, if thou be willing, remove this cup from me: nevertheless not my will, but thine, be done." (Luke 22:42.)

We cannot imagine the anguish of a loving Father, who, knowing what had to be done, accepted His Beloved Son's willingness to suffer for all mankind. In this agony Christ was not left alone. As if the Father were saying, "I cannot take it from you, but I can and will send you strength and peace," "there appeared an angel unto him from heaven, strengthening him." (Luke 22:43.)

If we, like the Savior, have the faith to put our trust in our Father in Heaven, to submit to His will, the true spirit of peace will come as a witness and strength that He *has* heard and answered our prayers.

If we resist the inspiration of God and turn from His promptings, we are left to our own confusion and lack of peace.

Sometimes, when our prayers are not answered as we desire, we may feel the Lord has rejected us or that our prayer was in vain. We may begin to doubt our worthiness before God, or even the reality and power of prayer. That is when we must continue to pray with patience and faith and to listen for that peace.

Following the incident when I was badly burned, I had felt with a surety that I would be healed. From the moment that first prayer was offered in my friend's home, I felt a comforting peace. While the doctor treated my burns, I hummed a hymn, finding comfort in these words:

> When sore trials came upon you,
> Did you think to pray? . . .

75

Oh, how praying rests the weary!
Prayer will change the night to day.
So, when life gets dark and dreary,
Don't forget to pray.
(*Hymns,* 1985, no. 140.)

Each day when the doctor changed my bandages, my mother would ask, "Can he see?" For many days the answer was the same: "No, not yet." Finally, when all the bandages were permanently removed, my eyesight began to return. I had anticipated that time with anxious expectation. The peace and comfort I had earlier felt gave me assurance that all would be well. However, when my vision cleared enough for me to see my hands and face, I was shocked, unprepared for what I saw. To my terrible disappointment, I found that all was *not* well. Seeing my scarred and disfigured skin brought great fear and doubt into my mind. I can remember thinking, Nothing can help this skin to be healed—not even the Lord.

Gratefully, as my prayers and the prayers of others continued, I felt the gifts of faith and of peace restored, and then, in time, my eyesight and my skin were healed. My friends who were injured were also blessed with complete recovery.

May we always seek to obtain the Lord's miraculous gift of peace through prayer. May we not forget to pray.

I join with Alma in saying: "May the peace of God rest upon you, . . . from this time forth and forever." (Alma 7:27.) With this testimony of peace through prayer, I bear witness of the reality of Jesus Christ and of His Father and of the Holy Ghost, who will lead our lives in the same *miraculous* way through answers to our prayers of faith.

Elder Rex D. Pinegar was called to serve in the First Council of the Seventy in 1972. He was sustained to the First Quorum of the Seventy in 1976.

PEACE THROUGH REPENTANCE

ELDER F. BURTON HOWARD

Let me ask you to picture two crystal goblets in your mind. They differ in size and shape. They are both of good quality and have been well used. One has been carefully kept in a china cupboard. It is clean and polished. It is warm and inviting in appearance. It sparkles in the light and is filled with clear water.

The other glass is coated with grime. It has not been in the dishpan for a long time. It has been used for purposes other than those for which it was made. Most recently it has been left outside in the weather and has served as a flowerpot. Although the flower is gone, it is still filled with dirt. It is dull and unbecoming in the light.

Is not each of us like a crystal glass? We vary in size and shape. Some of us radiate a special spirit. Some are dull and uninviting. Some fill the measure of their creation. Others do not. Each is filled with the accumulated experiences or debris of a lifetime.

Some contain mostly good things—clean thoughts, faith, and Christian service. These hold wisdom and peace. Others enclose dark and secret things. Over time they have been filled with unclean thoughts, selfishness, and sloth. They often hold doubt, contention, and unrest.

Many know they are not living up to their potential but for various reasons have procrastinated making changes in their lives. Some long for they know not what and spend their lives in a haphazard pursuit of happiness.

These, in a way, are like the crystal goblet which spent part of its existence filled with dirt. They sense that there is a higher purpose to things. They become dissatisfied and begin to search for meaning. First they look outside themselves. They sample the pleasures of the world. As they do they discover, much as did the snail who set out to look for its house, that after arriving at wherever they were going, they are no closer than before to the object of their search.

Ultimately, they look within. They have really known all the time that this was where to find peace. Sin, you see, is not just a state of mind. Wickedness never was and never will be happiness. (See Alma 41:10.) They discover that if they are not righteous they can never be happy. (See 2 Ne. 2:13.) They resolve to change. Then they are confronted, figuratively, with the problem of how to turn a weathered flowerpot into a sparkling crystal goblet. Questions are asked: Can I ever be forgiven? Is it really worth the effort? Where do I begin?

In the case of the glass it is easy to understand what to do. We begin by recognizing a better use for the crystal. A convenient place for dumping the unwanted contents is selected. The dirt is left there. The goblet is carefully washed with high quality detergent to remove the stains and residue. It is lovingly polished and placed once again in the company of other crystal glasses in the china cupboard. It is put back into use and cared for regularly.

There is a similar process whereby men and women are purified. The misuse of their lives is forgotten, and they are renewed and changed. This principle, of course, is repentance. When accompanied by authorized baptism, it provides not only an initial cleansing but an ongoing remission of sins as well. Participating in this purifying process is perhaps the most thrilling and important thing we can ever do. It has far-reaching, even eternal, consequences. Of more immediate interest, however, the rewards of repentance are peace and forgiveness in this present life.

Let me illustrate what all of this means. Some time ago I was asked to speak to a group of young men. I don't remember now exactly what was said, except that near the end I made the statement that no one, but no one, present had done anything for which he could not be forgiven.

After the meeting was over one of them came up to me and said, "I just have to talk to you." Inasmuch as I soon had another appointment, I asked if it could wait or if someone else could answer his question. He replied that he had already waited many years and that it was very important to him.

So taking advantage of the few minutes available, we found a little unused classroom, went in, and closed the door. "Did you really mean it? Did you?" he asked.

"Mean what?" I said.

"The part about how none of us had done anything that could not be forgiven," he replied.

"Of course I did," I said.

Through his tears his story came. He was of goodly parents. All of his life his mother had told him that he was going on a mission. Before he turned nineteen he was involved in a serious transgression. He didn't know how to tell his parents. He knew it would break their hearts. He knew that he wasn't worthy to serve a mission. In desperation, he began to look for an excuse not to go. He decided to take up smoking. He felt that his father could understand that better and would not probe for the real reason. Smoking would hurt his parents, he rationalized, but not as deeply as the truth.

He soon found, however, that the bishop wasn't put off by his use of tobacco. The bishop told him to just stop it and go on a mission anyway. So to get away from the bishop, he entered the military service. There he fell under the influence of some good Latter-day Saints. He stopped smoking. He was able to avoid major temptations. He served his time, received an honorable discharge, and returned home.

There was only one problem. He felt guilty. He had run away from a mission. He had run from the Lord and sensed somehow that gnawing discontent which comes when men do not live up to the purpose of their creation.

"So there you have it," he said. "I have not sinned again. I have attended my meetings. I keep the Word of Wisdom. Why is it that life seems empty? Why do I feel somehow that the Lord is displeased with me? How can I know for sure I have been forgiven?"

"Tell me what you know about repentance," I said.

He had obviously done some reading on the subject. He spoke of recognition, remorse, and restitution. He had resolved never to sin again.

"Let's see just how those principles apply to you," I said. "Let's begin with recognition. What is the best indicator that someone recognizes he has done wrong?"

"He will admit it," was his reply.

"To whom?" I asked.

He was thoughtful. "To himself, I guess."

"Men sometimes view themselves in a most favorable light," I said. "Wouldn't better evidence of awareness of wrongdoing be to tell someone else?"

"Yes, of course," he answered.

"Who else?" I insisted.

"Why, the person wronged," he said, "and . . . and maybe the bishop."

"Have you done this?" I asked.

"Not until now," he replied. "I've never told it all to anyone but you."

"Maybe that is why you have not ever felt completely forgiven," I responded.

He didn't say much.

"Let's look at the next step," I said. "What does it mean to feel remorse?"

"It means to be sorry," he answered.

"Are you sorry?" I asked.

"Oh yes," he said. "I feel as if I had wasted half my life." And his eyes filled again with tears.

"How sorry should you be?"

He looked puzzled. "What do you mean?"

I said, "Well, in order to be forgiven, a transgressor must experience godly sorrow. [See 2 Cor. 7:10.] He must have anguish of soul and genuine regret. This sorrow must be strong enough and long enough to motivate the additional processes of repentance, or it is not deep enough. Regret must be great enough so as to bring forth a changed person. That person must demonstrate that he is different than before by doing different and better things. Have you been sorry enough?" I asked again.

He hesitated. "I've changed," he said. "I'm not the same as I was before. I keep all the commandments now. I would like somehow to make it up to my parents. I have prayed for forgiveness. I apologized to the person I wronged. I realize the seriousness of what I have done. I would give anything if it hadn't happened. Maybe I haven't been as good as I could be, but I don't know what else to do. But I didn't ever confess to anyone."

I said, "I think after this meeting we can say you have even done that."

Then he said, "But after all of that, how can I ever know the Lord has really forgiven me?"

"That is the easy part," I replied. "When you have fully

repented, you feel an inner peace. You know somehow you are forgiven because the burden you have carried for so long, all of a sudden isn't there anymore. It is *gone* and you *know* it is gone."

He seemed doubtful still.

"I wouldn't be surprised," I said, "if when you leave this room, you discover that you have left much of your concern in here. If you have fully repented, the relief and the peace you feel will be so noticeable that it will be a witness to you that the Lord has forgiven you. If not today, I think it will happen soon."

I was late for my meeting. I opened the door and we went out together. I didn't know if we would ever meet again. The following Sunday evening, I received a telephone call at my home. It was from the young man.

"Brother Howard, how did you know?"

"How did I know what?" I asked.

"How did you know I would feel good about myself for the first time in five years?"

"Because the Lord promised he would remember no more," I said. (See Heb. 8:12.)

Then came the question: "Do you think the Church could use a twenty-four-year-old missionary? If they could, I would sure like to go."

Well, that young man was like one of the glasses we visualized. He had been out in the world and was partially filled with the wrong things. He was not content. Sin had clouded his vision and interfered with his potential. Until he could find a way to repent, he could never become what he knew he should be. It took time to change. It took prayer. It took effort, and it took help.

My young friend discovered that repentance is often a lonely, silent struggle. It is not a once-in-a-lifetime thing; rather, it lasts a lifetime. As President Stephen L Richards once said, it is an "ever-recurring acknowledgement of weakness and error and [a] seeking and living for the higher and better." (Conference Report, Apr. 1956, p. 91.)

This young man came to know that repentance is not a free gift. Just as faith without works is dead (see James 2:17), so repentance, too, demands much. It is not for the fainthearted or the lazy. It requires a complete turning away from wrongdoing and a set of new works or doings which produce a new heart and a different man. Repentance means work. It is not just stopping doing something. It is not just recognizing the wrong or knowing what should be done. It is not "a cycle of sinning and repenting and sinning again." (Hugh B. Brown, *Eternal Quest* [Salt Lake City: Bookcraft, 1956], p. 102.)

It is not only remorse; rather, it is an eternal principle which, when properly applied over sufficient time, always results in renewal, cleansing, and change.

This young man discovered that where sin is so serious as to jeopardize one's fellowship in the Church, the sinner must be willing to submit to the jurisdiction and judgment of the person who holds the custody of his Church membership and request forgiveness of him as well.

Most important of all, he learned that repentance is an indispensable counterpart to free agency. Free agency in the plan of salvation contemplates that men and women are free to choose the direction of their lives for themselves. Repentance means that as imperfect beings sometimes make imperfect decisions, they may correct their course. By following the rules of repentance, and through the atonement of Jesus Christ, mistakes don't count. The Lord agrees to "remember no more." (Heb. 8:12.) Because of the miraculous gift of forgiveness, transgressions are forgiven—*and forgotten*. Men can be cleansed and return to the path of purpose and progress and peace.

By repenting, my young friend became a new person. He was born again of the Spirit. He came to understand for himself, and that is the important thing, the meaning of the Savior's words: "Come unto me, all ye that labour and are heavy laden, and I will give you rest." (Matt. 11:28.)

Elder F. Burton Howard was called to serve as a member of the First Quorum of the Seventy in 1978.

THE CANKER
OF CONTENTION

ELDER RUSSELL M. NELSON

Some months ago my esteemed colleague Elder Carlos E. Asay and I stood atop Mount Nebo, where Moses once stood. (See Deut. 34:1–4.) We saw what he saw. In the distance to our right was the Sea of Galilee. The river Jordan flowed from there to the Dead Sea on our left. Ahead was the promised land into which Joshua led the Israelite faithful so long ago.

Later we were permitted to do what Moses could not. We were escorted from the Hashemite kingdom of Jordan to its western border with Israel. From there, we and our associates walked over the Allenby Bridge. We felt the tension as armed soldiers nearby guarded both sides of the international boundary.

After safely enduring this experience, I thought of the irony of it all. Here in the land made holy by the Prince of Peace, contention has existed almost continuously from that day to this.

Prior to His ascension from the Holy Land, the Savior pronounced a unique blessing: "Peace I leave with you, my peace I give unto you: not as the world giveth, give I unto you." (John 14:27.)

His peace is not necessarily political; His peace is personal. But that spirit of inner peace is driven away by contention.

85

Contention does not usually begin as strife between countries. More often, it starts with an individual, for we can contend within ourselves over simple matters of right and wrong. From there, contention can infect neighbors and nations like a spreading sore.

As we dread any disease that undermines the health of the body, so should we deplore contention, which is a corroding canker of the spirit. I appreciate the counsel of Abraham Lincoln, who said:

"Quarrel not at all. No man resolved to make the most of himself can spare time for personal contention. . . . Better give your path to a dog than be bitten by him." (Letter to J. M. Cutts, 26 Oct. 1863, in *Concise Lincoln Dictionary of Thoughts and Statements,* comp. and arr. Ralph B. Winn [New York: New York Philosophical Library, 1959], p. 107.)

President Ezra Taft Benson described contention as "another face of pride."

My concern is that contention is becoming accepted as a way of life. From what we see and hear in the media, the classroom, and the workplace, all are now infected to some degree with contention. How easy it is, yet how wrong it is, to allow habits of contention to pervade matters of spiritual significance, because contention is forbidden by divine decree:

"The Lord God hath commanded that men should not murder; that they should not lie; that they should not steal; that they should not take the name of the Lord their God in vain; that they should not envy; that they should not have malice; that they should not contend one with another." (2 Ne. 26:32.)

THE CREATOR OF CONTENTION

To understand why the Lord has commanded us not to "contend one with another," we must know the true source of contention. A Book of Mormon prophet revealed this important knowledge even before the birth of Christ:

"Satan did stir them up to do iniquity continually; yea, he did go about spreading rumors and contentions upon all the face of the land, that he might harden the hearts of the people against that which was good and against that which should come." (Hel. 16:22.)

When Christ did come to the Nephites, He confirmed that prophecy:

"He that hath the spirit of contention is not of me [saith the Lord], but is of the devil, who is the father of contention, and he stirreth up the hearts of men to contend with anger, one with another. Behold, this is not my doctrine, to stir up the hearts of men with anger, one against another; but this is my doctrine, that such things should be done away." (3 Ne.11:29–30.)

THE ORIGIN OF CONTENTION

Contention existed before the earth was formed. When God's plan for creation and mortal life on the earth was first announced, sons and daughters of God shouted for joy. The plan was dependent on man's agency, his subsequent fall from the presence of God, and the merciful provision of a Savior to redeem mankind. Scriptures reveal that Lucifer sought vigorously to *amend* the plan by destroying the agency of man. Satan's cunning motive was unmasked in his statement:

"Behold, here am I, send me, I will be thy son, and I will redeem all mankind, that one soul shall not be lost, and surely I will do it; wherefore give me thine honor." (Moses 4:1.)

Satan's selfish efforts to alter the plan of God resulted in great contention in heaven. The Prophet Joseph Smith explained:

"Jesus said there would be certain souls that would not be saved; and the devil said he could save them all, and laid his plans before the grand council, who gave their vote in favor of

87

Jesus Christ. So the devil rose up in rebellion against God, and was cast down." (*Teachings of the Prophet Joseph Smith*, sel. Joseph Fielding Smith [Salt Lake City: Deseret Book Co., 1938], p. 357.)

This war in heaven was not a war of bloodshed. It was a war of conflicting ideas—the beginning of contention.

Scriptures repeatedly warn that the father of contention opposes the plan of our Heavenly Father. Satan's method relies on the infectious canker of contention. Satan's motive: to gain personal acclaim even over God Himself.

TARGETS OF THE ADVERSARY

The work of the adversary may be likened to loading guns in opposition to the work of God. Salvos containing germs of contention are aimed and fired at strategic targets essential to that holy work. These vital targets include—in addition to the individual—the family, leaders of the Church, and divine doctrine.

THE FAMILY

The family has been under attack ever since Satan first taunted Adam and Eve. (See Gen. 3; Moses 4.) So today, each must guard against the hazard of contention in the family. It usually begins innocently. Years ago when our daughters were little girls who wanted to be big girls, the style of the day was to wear multiple petticoats. A little contention could have crept in as the girls soon learned that the one to get dressed first was the one best dressed.

In a large family of boys, those with the longest reach were the best fed. In order to avoid obvious contention, they adopted a rule that required them at mealtime to leave at least one foot on the floor.

The home is the great laboratory of learning and love. Here

parents help children overcome these natural tendencies to be selfish. In rearing our own family, Sister Nelson and I have been very grateful for this counsel from the Book of Mormon:

"Ye will not suffer your children that they go hungry, or naked; neither will ye suffer that they transgress the laws of God, and fight and quarrel one with another. . . . But ye will teach them to walk in the ways of truth and soberness; ye will teach them to love one another, and to serve one another." (Mosiah 4:14–15.)

And I might add, please be patient while children learn those lessons.

Parents should be partners to cherish and protect one another, knowing that the aim of the adversary is to destroy the integrity of the family.

LEADERS OF THE CHURCH

Leaders of the Church are targets for attack by those who stir contention. This is true even though not a single leader has called himself or herself to a position of responsibility. Each General Authority, for instance, chose another path to pursue as his life's occupation. But the reality is, as with Peter or Paul, each was surely "called of God, by prophecy, and by the laying on of hands by those who are in authority." (Articles of Faith 1:5.) With that call comes the commitment to emulate the patterns of the Prince of Peace.

That goal is shared by worthy servants of the Master, who would not speak ill of the Lord's anointed nor provoke contention over teachings declared by ancient or living prophets.

Certainly no faithful follower of God would promote any cause even remotely related to religion if rooted in controversy, because contention is not of the Lord.

Surely a stalwart would not lend his or her good name to

periodicals, programs, or forums that feature offenders who do sow "discord among brethren." (Prov. 6:19; see also 6:14.)

Such agitators unfortunately fulfill long-foretold prophecy: they "take counsel together, against the Lord, and against his anointed." (Ps. 2:2.)

Yet, mercifully, the anointed pray for those who attack them, knowing the sad fate prophesied for their attackers. (See D&C 121:16–22.)

Throughout the world, Saints of the Lord follow Him *and* His anointed leaders. They have learned that the path of dissent leads to real dangers. The Book of Mormon carries this warning:

"Now these dissenters, having the same instruction and the same information . . . , having been instructed in the same knowledge of the Lord, nevertheless, it is strange to relate, not long after their dissensions they became more hardened and impenitent, and more wild, wicked and ferocious . . . ; giving way to indolence, and all manner of lasciviousness; yea, entirely forgetting the Lord their God." (Alma 47:36.)

How divisive is the force of dissension! Small acts can lead to such great consequences. Regardless of position or situation, no one can safely assume immunity to contention's terrible toll.

Thomas B. Marsh, once one of the Twelve, left the Church. His spiritual slide to apostasy started because his wife and another woman had quarreled over a little cream! After an absence from the Church of nearly nineteen years, he came back. To a congregation of Saints, he then said:

"If there are any among this people who should ever apostatize and do as I have done, prepare your backs for a good whipping, if you are such as the Lord loves. But if you will take my advice, you will stand by the authorities." (*Journal of Discourses*, 26 vols. [Liverpool, England: Albert Carrington and others, 1853–1886], 5:206; see also Gordon B. Hinckley, *Ensign*, May 1984, pp. 81–83.)

Of course the authorities are human. But to them God has entrusted the keys to His divine work. And He holds us accountable for our responses to the teachings of His servants. These are the words of the Lord:

"If my people will hearken unto my voice, and unto the voice of my servants whom I have appointed to lead my people, behold, verily I say unto you, they shall not be moved out of their place. But if they will not hearken to my voice, nor unto the voice of these men whom I have appointed, they shall not be blest." (D&C 124:45–46.)

DIVINE DOCTRINE

Divine doctrine of the Church is the prime target of attack by the spiritually contentious. Well do I remember a friend who would routinely sow seeds of contention in Church classes. His assaults would invariably be preceded by this predictable comment: "Let me play the role of devil's advocate." Recently he passed away. One day he will stand before the Lord in judgment. Then, I wonder, will my friend's predictable comment again be repeated?

Such contentious spirits are not new. In an epistle to Timothy, the Apostle Paul gave this warning, "that the name of God and his doctrine be not blasphemed." (1 Tim. 6:1.)

"If any man teach otherwise, and consent not to wholesome words, even the words of our Lord Jesus Christ, and to [his] doctrine . . . doting about questions and strifes of words, . . . supposing that gain is godliness: from such withdraw thyself." (1 Tim. 6:3–5; see also Isa. 29:21; 2 Ne. 27:32; D&C 19:30; 38:41; 60:14.)

Dissecting doctrine in a controversial way in order to draw attention to oneself is not pleasing to the Lord. He declared:

"Bring to light the true points of my doctrine, yea, and the only doctrine which is in me. And this I do that I may establish my gospel, that there may not be so much contention; yea, Satan doth stir up the hearts of the people to contention concerning the points of my doctrine; and in these things they do err, for they do wrest the scriptures and do not understand them." (D&C 10:62–63.)

Contention fosters disunity. The Book of Mormon teaches the better way:

"Alma, having authority from God, . . . commanded them that there should be no contention one with another, but that they should look forward with one eye, having one faith and one baptism, having their hearts knit together in unity and in love one towards another." (Mosiah 18:18, 21; see also 23:15.)

STEPS TO SUPPLANT CONTENTION

What can we do to combat this canker of contention? What steps may each of us take to supplant the spirit of contention with a spirit of personal peace?

To begin, show compassionate concern for others. Control the tongue, the pen, and the word processor. Whenever tempted to dispute, remember this proverb: "He that is void of wisdom despiseth his neighbour: but a man of understanding holdeth his peace." (Prov. 11:12; see also 17:28.)

Bridle the passion to speak or write contentiously for personal gain or glory. The Apostle Paul thus counseled the Philippians, "Let nothing be done through strife or vainglory; but in lowliness of mind let each esteem other better than themselves." (Philip. 2:3.)

Such high mutual regard would then let us respectfully disagree without being disagreeable.

But the ultimate step lies beyond beginning control of expression. Personal peace is reached when one, in humble submissiveness, truly loves God. Heed carefully this scripture:

"There was no contention in the land, *because of* the love of

God which did dwell in the hearts of the people." (4 Ne. 1:15; italics added; see also 1:2.)

Thus, love of God should be our aim. It is the first commandment—the foundation of faith. As we develop love of God and Christ, love of family and neighbor will naturally follow. Then will we eagerly emulate Jesus. He healed. He comforted. He taught, "Blessed are the peacemakers: for they shall be called the children of God." (Matt. 5:9; see also 3 Ne. 12:9.)

Through love of God, the pain caused by the fiery canker of contention will be extinguished from the soul. This healing begins with a personal vow: "Let there be peace on earth, and let it begin with me." (Sy Miller and Jill Jackson, "Let There Be Peace on Earth," © Jan-Lee Music, Beverly Hills, Calif., 1972.) This commitment will then spread to family and friends and will bring peace to neighborhoods and nations.

Shun contention. Seek godliness. Be enlightened by eternal truth. Be like-minded with the Lord in love and united with Him in faith. Then shall "the peace of God, which passeth all understanding" (Philip. 4:7) be yours, to bless you and your posterity through generations yet to come.

Elder Russell M. Nelson was ordained an Apostle in 1984.

Peace: A Triumph of Principles

Elder Marvin J. Ashton

Many years ago I heard a story that impressed me. A beautiful little blind girl was sitting on the lap of her father in a crowded compartment in a train. A friend seated nearby said to the father, "Let me give you a little rest," and he reached over and took the little girl on his lap.

A few moments later the father said to her, "Do you know who is holding you?"

"No," she replied, "but you do."

Some might be inclined to say, "What a perfect trust this child had in her father." Others may say, "What a wonderful example of love." And still others might say, "What an example of faith." To me it indicates a beautiful blending of all of these principles, which brought a priceless inner peace to the child. She knew she was safe because she knew her father *knew* who was holding her. Affection, respect, and care over the years had placed in this little girl's heart a peace that surpasseth all understanding. She was at peace because she knew and trusted her father.

We plead for peace in our prayers and thoughts. Where is peace? Can we ever enjoy this great gift while wars, rumors of wars, discord, evil, and contention swirl all around us? The answer is yes. Just as the little blind girl sat on the stranger's lap with perfect contentment because her father knew him, so we can learn to know our Father and find inner peace as we live his principles.

It is very significant that when Jesus came forth from the tomb and appeared to his disciples, his first greeting was, "Peace be unto you." (Luke 24:36.) Peace—not passion, not personal possessions, not personal accomplishments nor happiness—is one of the greatest blessings a man can receive. Our trust and our relationship with our Heavenly Father should be one similar to that of the little blind girl and her earthly father. When sorrow, tragedy, and heartbreaks occur in our lives, wouldn't it be comforting if when the whisperings of God say, "Do you know why this has happened to you?" we could have the peace of mind to answer, "No, but you do."

Certainly peace is the opposite of fear. Peace is a blessing that comes to those who trust in God. It is established through individual righteousness. True personal peace comes about through eternal vigilance and constant righteous efforts. No man can be at peace who is untrue to his better self. No man can have lasting peace who is living a lie. Peace can never come to the transgressor of the law. Commitment to God's laws is the basis for peace. Peace is something we earn. It is not a gift. Rather, it is a possession earned by those who love God and work to achieve the blessings of peace. It is not a written document. It is something that must come from within.

The Salt Lake Valley was settled by those who trekked over the plains under extremely difficult conditions so they could worship God in peace. Left behind was Nauvoo, a deserted city desecrated by the uninformed, misinformed, embittered enemies of the Church. Peace had flown from the City Beautiful. What a price some of those who have gone before us have paid for the privilege of worshiping in peace.

Never will peace and hatred be able to abide in the same soul. Permanent peace will elude those individuals or groups whose objective is to condemn, discredit, rail at, or tear down those whose beliefs are different from their own. These people live by hatred and would destroy others insofar as it is in their power to do so. True Christians have no time for contention. Lasting peace cannot be built while we are reviling or hating others. Those who preach hate, ridicule, and untruths cannot be classified as peacemakers. Until they repent they will reap the harvest to which those engaged in the business of hatred are entitled. Feelings of enmity and malice can never be compatible with feelings of peace.

"The wicked are like the troubled sea, when it cannot rest, whose waters cast up mire and dirt. There is no peace, saith my God, to the wicked." (Isa. 57:20–21.)

However, only those at peace can properly cope with accusations and slander. Inner peace is the prized possession of God's valiant. A testimony of the truthfulness of the teachings of our Savior gives personal peace in times of adversity.

There are those who dangle false enticements of peace before us. These are they who are greedy and power hungry. "Be not deceived; God is not mocked: . . . He that soweth to his flesh shall of the flesh reap corruption." (Gal. 6:7–8.) Inner peace flees from those who sacrifice virtue for sexual promiscuity. There are some who advocate and promote new sexual exploits under the guise of "relief from stress." These people are only sowing unto the flesh and peddling devilish deeds. Wickedness, no matter how it is labeled or camouflaged, will eventually bring grief and heartache and wipe out inner peace.

Peace will never be the possession of those who participate in vulgar conversations and behavior. Let us not be planters of poisonous seeds. Rather let us nourish roots of peace in the soil of righteous principles.

It was Ralph Waldo Emerson who declared the mighty truth, "Nothing can bring you peace but yourself. Nothing can bring you peace but a triumph of principles." ("Self-Reliance," in *Ralph Waldo Emerson: Essays and Lectures* [New York: The Library of America, 1983], p. 282.)

Peace is not a purchase away. Peace is not when the final installment is paid. Peace is not when marriage comes nor when all the children are enrolled in school. Peace is not when the last child returns from the mission field. Peace is not when an inheritance is received. Peace is not when the scars of death start to heal.

True peace must not be dependent upon conditions or happenings. Peace must stem from an inward contentment built upon trust, faith, and goodwill toward God, fellowmen, and self. It must be constantly nurtured by the individual who is soundly anchored to the gospel of Jesus Christ. Only then can a person realize that the trials and tribulations of daily life are less important than God's total goodness.

Lasting peace is an eternal personal quest. Peace does come from obedience to the law. Peace comes to those who develop character and trust.

We have a young grandson who loves gymnastics. He is progressing well and delights in showing us what he can do. While he develops these performance skills his body is maturing in limberness and strength. The last time he invited me to feel the muscles in his arms, I congratulated him. I was proud. As he jumped away from me (gymnasts, it seems, are always jumping and springing), I was impressed with the thought that his parents, grandparents, teachers, and others have an obligation to teach him one of life's great truths. Flabbiness of character should always be more of a concern than flabbiness of muscles. Body building and body conditioning are worthwhile goals, but there is more needed to gain true inner peace. We must blend balance in our lives and increase in wisdom and stature, and in favor with God and man (see Luke 2:52) to reach our full potential.

No peace will be lasting unless it is built upon the solid foundation of eternal principles such as love of God, love of neighbor, and love of self. Those who love their neighbors can bring peace and happiness to many. Love can build bridges to understanding and tear down walls of suspicion and hate. Christlike love can bring peace into any neighborhood. With that kind of love each of us can help resolve petty differences, be they in the home or community.

While living in another nation just before World War II was to begin, a leading government official had been working hard to maintain peace for his country. He had in his hands a signed document guaranteeing peace. After negotiating in good faith, he seemingly had achieved that for which millions of his countrymen had been hoping and praying. He publicly assured all of us that it was peace for our times.

Soon, however, he realized that he had been deceived. The men with whom he had negotiated were selfish, greedy, and power hungry. They were only bargaining for time to solidify their position. War came.

We learned that peace can never be achieved when we deal with those who deceive and ignore the basic principles taught by our Savior.

At such times external events make it even more imperative that we seek peace within ourselves. It is futile to seek it from outward sources.

It was George C. Marshall who wisely said, "We must take the nations of the world as they are, the human passions and prejudices of people as they exist, and find some way to secure . . . a peaceful world."

Peace must be a triumph of principles. Selfishness and lack

of patience seem to block the way. We cry out today with urgency, "Have mercy, O Lord, upon all the nations of the earth; have mercy upon the rulers of our land; may those principles, which were so honorably and nobly defended, namely, the Constitution of our land, by our fathers, be established forever." (D&C 109:54.) The respected Winston Churchill once said, "The day will come when . . . victorious nations will plan and build in justice and freedom a house of many mansions, where there will be room for all."

We pray earnestly that all leaders of nations, large and small, free or oppressed, would know: "And above all things, clothe yourselves with the bond of charity, as with a mantle, which is the bond of perfectness and peace." (D&C 88:125.)

Despite the challenges of curbing federal budget deficits and riots and terrorism, of controlling inflation, and of [maintaining international relations], thank God America is at peace. Thank God for those other nations who teach and live in peace. Thank God for worthy men who work to keep it that way. Our responsibility as a nation and its people is to continue to take the lead in furthering peace on earth and goodwill toward all men. (See Luke 2:14.) To all mankind worldwide who would anxiously engage themselves in lasting peace, we share: "But learn that he who doeth the works of righteousness shall receive his reward, even peace in this world, and eternal life in the world to come." (D&C 59:23.)

The individual, the home, the Church, the school, the government are the fundamental institutions upon which lasting peace depends. The main purpose of schools must always be to develop character, to develop loyalty to the government, loyalty to the home, and loyalty to the individual. This is what real peace is all about—internal and external. No peace, even though temporarily achieved, will be lasting unless it is built upon the solid foundation of such eternal principles as love of God, love of neighbor, love of self. Most men yearn for peace, cry for peace, pray for peace, and work for peace, but there will not be lasting peace until all mankind follow the path pointed out and walked by the living Christ. There can be no peace in sin and disobedience. If I do not have peace within me, others around me will suffer.

God has a special love for those of his children who promote and advocate peace. Our responsibility as Church members is to instill in an ever-growing number of people the fact that our personal attitudes and behavior can bring a measure of peace to our troubled world and a sense of stability to anxious times. With peace in our hearts we can know that the trends of the world and the criticisms of men cannot alter the truths of God.

When we properly blend into our lives true principles of love, honesty, respect, character, faith, and patience, peace will become our priceless possession. Peace is a triumph of correct principles.

Just as the little girl could sit peacefully on the stranger's lap because her father knew him, so we can find peace if we know our Father and learn to live by his principles.

None of us will avoid the storms of life. The winds and the waves will periodically interfere with our chosen course. The laws of the gospel can bring us back on course and guide us to peaceful waters.

Elder Marvin J. Ashton was called to be a General Authority in 1969, was ordained an Apostle in 1971, and died in 1994.

PART 3

FINDING PEACE
IN ADVERSITY

"MASTER, THE TEMPEST IS RAGING"

PRESIDENT HOWARD W. HUNTER

North of Jerusalem about eighty miles or so lies a beautiful body of water known earlier in biblical times as the Sea of Chinneroth and the Lake of Gennesaret, but known best to us today as the Sea of Galilee. It is a freshwater inland lake a little over twelve miles long and seven miles wide. The river Jordan flows through it, from north to south, on its journey toward the Dead Sea.

This was the lake Jesus knew as a child and as a young man, its western shores lying just twelve or fifteen miles from his boyhood home of Nazareth. It was to this lake and the neighboring Galilean hills that Jesus returned so often during those demanding years of his public ministry.

On one journey to Galilee, the Savior taught the multitudes crowded near the water's edge. With the people pressing ever closer, Jesus sought a better teaching circumstance by stepping into a boat and pushing out a few yards into the sea. There, a short distance from the eager crowd, he could be seen and heard by those straining for sight and words of the Master.

Following his discourse, the Savior invited his disciples to join him, and they set out together for the other side of the lake. The Sea of Galilee is quite low, about 680 feet below sea level, and the heat becomes quite great. The hills surrounding the water rise up very sharply and to considerable height. The cold air rushing down from the hills meets the warm air rising from the lake in such a way that sudden and temporarily violent storms can occur on the surface of that inland sea. It was just such a storm as this that Jesus and his disciples found as they crossed the lake at evening time. This is the way Mark described it:

"And when they had sent away the multitude, they took him even as he was in the ship. And there were also with him other little ships.

"And there arose a great storm of wind, and the waves beat into the ship, so that it was now full.

"And he was in the hinder part of the ship, asleep on a pillow: and they awake him, and say unto him, Master, carest thou not that we perish?

"And he arose, and rebuked the wind, and said unto the sea, Peace, be still. And the wind ceased, and there was a great calm.

"And he said unto them, Why are ye so fearful? how is it that ye have no faith?

"And they feared exceedingly, and said one to another, What manner of man is this, that even the wind and the sea obey him?" (Mark 4:36–41.)

All of us have seen some sudden storms in our lives. A few of them, though temporary like these on the Sea of Galilee, can be violent and frightening and potentially destructive. As individuals, as families, as communities, as nations, even as a Church, we have had sudden squalls arise which have made us ask one way or another, "Master, carest thou not that we perish?" And one way or another we always hear in the stillness after the storm, "Why are ye so fearful? how is it that ye have no faith?"

None of us would like to think we have *no* faith, but I suppose the Lord's gentle rebuke here is largely deserved. This great Jehovah, in whom we say we trust and whose name we have taken upon us, is he who said, "Let there be a firmament in the midst of the waters, and let it divide the waters from the waters." (Gen. 1:6.) And he is also the one who said, "Let the waters under the heaven be gathered together unto one place, and let the dry land appear." (Gen. 1:9.) Furthermore, it was he who parted the Red Sea, allowing the Israelites to pass through on dry ground. (See Ex. 14:21–22.) Certainly it should be no surprise that he could command a few elements acting up on the Sea of Galilee. And our faith should remind us that he can calm the troubled waters of our lives.

Let me recall for you the story of Mary Ann Baker. Her beloved and only brother suffered from the same respiratory disease that had taken their parents' lives, and he left their home in Chicago to find a warmer climate in the southern part of the United States.

For a time he seemed to be improving, but then a sudden turn in his health came and he died almost immediately. Mary Ann and her sister were heartbroken. It only added to their deep grief that neither their own health nor their personal finances allowed them to claim their brother's body or to finance its return to Chicago for burial.

The Baker family had been raised as faithful Christians, but Mary's trust in a loving God broke under the strain of her brother's death and her own diminished circumstances. "God does not care for me or mine," said Mary Ann. "This particular manifestation of what they call 'divine providence' is unworthy of a God of love." Does that sound at all familiar?

"I have always tried to believe on Christ and give the Master a consecrated life," she said, "but this is more than I can bear. What have I done to deserve this? What have I left undone that God should wreak His vengeance upon me in this way?" (Ernest K. Emurian, *Living Stories of Famous Hymns* [Boston: W. A. Widdle Co., 1955], pp. 83–85.)

I suppose we have all had occasion, individually or collectively, to cry out on some stormy sea, "Master, carest thou not that we perish?" And so cried Mary Ann Baker.

But as the days and the weeks went by, the God of life and love began to calm the winds and the waves of what this sweet young woman called "her unsanctified heart." Her faith not only returned but it flourished, and like Job of old, she learned new things, things "too wonderful" to have known before her despair. On the Sea of Galilee, the stirring of the disciples' faith was ultimately more important than the stilling of the sea, and so it was with her.

Later, as something of a personal testimonial and caring very much for the faith of others who would be tried by personal despair, she wrote the words of the hymn we have all sung, "Master, the Tempest Is Raging":

> Master, the tempest is raging!
> The billows are tossing high!
> The sky is o'ershadowed with blackness.
> No shelter or help is nigh.
>
> Carest thou not that we perish?
> How canst thou lie asleep
> When each moment so madly is threatening
> A grave in the angry deep? . . .
>
> Master, with anguish of spirit
> I bow in my grief today.
> The depths of my sad heart are troubled.
> Oh, waken and save, I pray!
>
> Torrents of sin and of anguish
> Sweep o'er my sinking soul,
> And I perish! I perish! dear Master.
> Oh, hasten and take control!

Then this beautiful, moving refrain:

The winds and the waves shall obey thy will:
Peace, be still, peace, be still.
Whether the wrath of the storm-tossed sea
Or demons or men or whatever it be,
No waters can swallow the ship where lies
The Master of ocean and earth and skies.

They all shall sweetly obey thy will.
Peace, be still; peace, be still.
They all shall sweetly obey thy will.
Peace, peace, be still.

Too often, I fear, both in the living of life and in the singing of this hymn, we fail to emphasize the sweet peace of this concluding verse:

Master, the terror is over.
The elements sweetly rest.
Earth's sun in the calm lake is mirrored,
And heaven's within my breast.

Linger, O blessed Redeemer!
Leave me alone no more,
And with joy I shall make the blest harbor
And rest on the blissful shore.
(*Hymns,* 1985, no. 105.)

We will all have some adversity in our lives. I think we can be reasonably sure of that. Some of it will have the potential to be violent and damaging and destructive. Some of it may even strain our faith in a loving God who has the power to administer relief in our behalf.

To those anxieties I think the Father of us all would say, "Why are ye so fearful? how is it that ye have no faith?" And of course that has to be faith for the whole journey, the entire experience, the fulness of our life, not simply around the bits and pieces and tempestuous moments. At the end of the journey, an

109

end none of us can see now, we will say, "Master, the terror is over. . . . Linger, Oh, blessed Redeemer! Leave me alone no more."

Jesus said, "In the world ye shall have tribulation: but be of good cheer; I have overcome the world." (John 16:33.) On the same occasion, he said, "Peace I leave with you, my peace I give unto you: not as the world giveth, give I unto you." (John 14:27.) Throughout his life and ministry he spoke of peace, and when he came forth from the tomb and appeared unto his disciples, his first greeting was, "Peace be unto you." (John 20:19.)

But Jesus was not spared grief and pain and anguish and buffeting. No tongue can speak the unutterable burden he carried, nor have we the wisdom to understand the prophet Isaiah's description of him as "a man of sorrows." (Isa. 53:3.) His ship was tossed most of his life, and, at least to mortal eyes, it crashed fatally on the rocky coast of Calvary. We are asked not to look on life with mortal eyes; with spiritual vision we know something quite different was happening upon the cross.

Peace was on the lips and in the heart of the Savior no matter how fiercely the tempest was raging. May it so be with us—in our own hearts, in our own homes, in our nations of the world, and even in the buffetings faced from time to time by the Church. We should not expect to get through life individually or collectively without some opposition.

One of the wisest of the ancient Romans once spoke a great gospel truth and probably never realized he had done so. Speaking of Roman naval power and the absolute imperative to control the oceans, Cicero said to a military aide, "He who commands the sea has command of everything." (See W. Gurney Benham, *Putnam's Complete Book of Quotations* [New York: G. P. Putnam's Sons, 1926], p. 505.) Of that I so testify.

"Whether the wrath of the storm-tossed sea or demons or men or whatever it be, no waters can swallow the ship where lies the Master of ocean and earth and skies. They all shall sweetly obey [his] will. Peace, be still!"

President Howard W. Hunter was ordained an Apostle in 1959, was sustained President of the Church in 1994, and died in 1995.

FINDING PEACE "NOTWITHSTANDING MY WEAKNESS"

ELDER NEAL A. MAXWELL

I speak, not to the slackers in the Kingdom, but to those who carry their own load and more; not to those lulled into false security, but to those buffeted by false insecurity, who, though laboring devotedly in the Kingdom, have recurring feelings of falling forever short.

Earlier disciples who heard Jesus preach some exacting doctrines were also anxious and said, "Who then can be saved?" (Mark 10:26.)

The first thing to be said of this feeling of inadequacy is that it is normal. There is no way the Church can honestly describe where we must yet go and what we must yet do without creating a sense of immense distance. Following celestial road signs while in telestial traffic jams is not easy, especially when we are not just moving next door—or even across town.

In a Kingdom where perfection is an eventual expectation, each other's needs for improvement have a way of being noticed. Perceptive Jethro had plenty of data to back up the crisp counsel he gave his son-in-law Moses. (See Exod. 18.) Even prophets notice their weaknesses. Nephi persisted in a major task

113

"notwithstanding my weakness." (2 Ne. 33:11.) Another Nephite prophet, Jacob, wrote candidly of his "over anxiety" for those with whom he was not certain he could communicate adequately. (Jac. 4:18.) Each of our modern prophets have met those telling moments when they have felt as if they could not meet a challenge. Yet they did.

Thus the feelings of inadequacy are common. So are the feelings of fatigue; hence, the needed warning about our becoming weary of well-doing. (See D&C 64:33.)

The scriptural advice, "Do not run faster or labor more than you have strength" (D&C 10:4) suggests paced progress, much as God used seven creative periods in preparing man and this earth. There is a difference, therefore, between being "anxiously engaged" (D&C 58:27) and being over-anxious and thus underengaged.

Some of us who would not chastise a neighbor for his frailties have a field day with our own. Some of us stand before no more harsh a judge than ourselves, a judge who stubbornly refuses to admit much happy evidence and who cares nothing for due process. Fortunately the Lord loves us more than we love ourselves. A constructive critic truly cares for that which he criticizes, including himself, whereas self-pity is the most condescending form of pity; it soon cannibalizes all other concerns.

The scriptures are like a developmental display window through which we can see gradual growth—along with this vital lesson: it is direction first, *then* velocity! Enoch's unique people were improved "in process of time." (Moses 7:21.) Jesus "received not of the fulness at first, but received grace for grace" (D&C 93:12) and even He grew and "increased in wisdom and stature" (Luke 2:52).

In the scriptural display window we see Lehi struggling as an anxious and "trembling parent." (2 Ne. 1:14.) We see sibling rivalries but also deep friendships like that of David and Jonathan. We see that all conflict is not catastrophe. We view misunderstandings even in rich relationships like that of Paul and Barnabas. We see a prophet candidly reminding King Saul that there was a time when "thou wast little in thine own sight." (1 Sam. 15:17.)

We see our near-perfect parents, Adam and Eve, coping with challenges in the first family, for their children, too, came trailing traits from their formative first estate.

We see a legalistic Paul, but later read his matchless sermon on charity. (See 1 Cor. 13.) We see a jailed John the Baptist—and there had been no greater prophet (Matt. 11:11)—needing reassurance (see Matt. 11:2–4). We see Peter walking briefly on water but requiring rescue from Jesus' outstretched hand (see Matt. 14:25–31); later we see Peter stretching his strong hand to Tabitha after helping to restore her to life (see Acts 9:36–42).

Moroni was not the first underinformed leader to conclude that another leader was not doing enough. (See Alma 60.) Nor was Pahoran's sweet, generous response to his "beloved brother" Moroni the last such that will be needed. (See Alma 61.)

What can we do to manage these vexing feelings of inadequacy? Here are but a few suggestions:

1. We can distinguish more clearly between divine discontent and the devil's dissonance, between dissatisfaction with self and disdain for self. We need the first and must shun the second, remembering that when conscience calls to us from the next ridge, it is not solely to scold but also to beckon.

2. We can contemplate how far we have already come in the climb along the pathway to perfection; it is usually much farther than we acknowledge. True, we *are* "unprofitable servants," but partly because when "we have done that which was our duty to do" (Luke 17:10), with every ounce of such obedience comes a bushel of blessings.

3. We can accept help as well as gladly give it. Happily, General Naaman received honest but helpful feedback, not from fellow generals but from his orderlies. (See 2 Kings 5:1–14.) In

the economy of heaven, God does not send thunder if a still, small voice is enough, or a prophet if a priest can do the job.

4. We can allow for the agency of others (including our children) *before* we assess our adequacy. Often our deliberate best is less effectual because of someone else's worst.

5. We can write down, and act upon, more of those accumulating resolutions for self-improvement that we so often leave, unrecovered, at the edge of sleep.

6. We can admit that if we were to die today, we would be genuinely and deeply missed. Perhaps parliaments would not praise us, but no human circle is so small that it does not touch another, and another.

7. We can put our hand to the plow, looking neither back nor around, comparatively. Our gifts and opportunities differ; some are more visible and impactful. We all have *at least* one gift *and* an open invitation to seek "earnestly the best gifts." (D&C 46:8.)

8. We can make quiet but more honest inventories of our strengths, since, in this connection, most of us are dishonest bookkeepers and need confirming "outside auditors." He who was thrust down in the first estate delights to have us put ourselves down. Self-contempt is of Satan; there is none of it in heaven. We should, of course, learn from our mistakes, but without forever studying the instant replays as if these were the game of life itself.

9. We can add to each other's storehouse of self-esteem by giving deserved, specific commendation more often, remembering, too, that those who are breathless from going the second mile need deserved praise just as the fallen need to be lifted up.

10. We can also keep moving. Only the Lord can compare crosses, but all crosses are easier to carry when we keep moving. Men finally climbed Mount Everest, not by standing at its base in consuming awe, but by shouldering their packs and by placing one foot in front of another. Feet are made to move forward—not backward!

11. We can know that when we have *truly* given what we have, it is like paying a full tithe; it is, in that respect, *all* that was asked. The widow who cast in her two mites was neither self-conscious nor searching for mortal approval.

12. We can allow for the reality that God is more concerned with growth than with geography. Thus, those who marched in Zion's Camp were not exploring the Missouri countryside but their own possibilities.

13. We can learn that at the center of our agency is our freedom to form a healthy attitude toward whatever circumstances we are placed in! Those, for instance, who stretch themselves in service—though laced with limiting diseases—are often the healthiest among us! The Spirit *can* drive the flesh beyond where the body first agrees to go!

14. Finally, we can accept this stunning, irrevocable truth: Our Lord can lift us from deep despair and cradle us midst any care. We cannot tell Him *anything* about aloneness *or* nearness!

Yes, this is a gospel of grand expectations, but God's grace is sufficient for each of us. *Discouragement is not the absence of adequacy but the absence of courage,* and our personal progress should be yet another way we witness to the wonder of it all!

True, there are no *instant* Christians, but there are *constant* Christians!

If we so live, we too can say in personal prospectus, "And I soon go to the place of my rest, which is with my Redeemer; for . . . *then shall I see his face* with pleasure" (Enos 1:27; italics added), for then will our confidence *"wax strong in the presence of God"* (D&C 121:45; italics added), and He who cannot lie will attest to our adequacy with the warm words "Well done."

Elder Neal A. Maxwell was called as a General Authority in 1976, and was ordained an Apostle in 1981.

"WOMAN, WHY WEEPEST THOU?"

PRESIDENT JAMES E. FAUST

Today I speak to those who have heart-rending challenges. I speak to those who suffer, to those who mourn and have heartaches. I speak to those with physical, mental, or emotional pain. I speak to those born crippled or who have become crippled. I speak to those who were born blind or who can no longer see the sunsets. I speak to those who have never been able or who are no longer able to hear a bird sing. I speak to those who have the privileged responsibility of helping others who have mental and physical disabilities. I also speak to those who may be in serious transgression.

I take as my text the words of the Savior to the sorrowing Mary Magdalene who "stood without at the sepulchre weeping." (John 20:11.) As she turned around she "saw Jesus standing, and knew not that it was Jesus.

"Jesus saith unto her, Woman, why weepest thou?" (John 20:14–15.) The Savior was speaking not just to the sorrowing Mary. He was also speaking to us—men, women, and children, and all of mankind ever born or yet to be born, for tears of sorrow, pain, or remorse are the common lot of mankind.

The complexities of this life at times tend to be very dehumanizing and overwhelming. Some have so much, while others struggle with so very little.

It is a joy to meet with the faithful Saints of the Church all over the world. Even though some of them have difficulties and challenges and lack material wealth, yet they seem to find much happiness and are able to walk in faith over the rough cobblestones of life. Their deep faith strengthens ours as we meet with them.

Many who think that life is unfair do not see things within the larger vision of what the Savior did for us through the atonement and the resurrection. Each of us has at times agony, heartbreak, and despair when we must, like Job, reach deep down inside to the bedrock of our own faith. The depth of our belief in the resurrection and the atonement of the Savior will, I believe, determine the measure of courage and purpose with which we meet life's challenges.

The first words of the risen Lord to His disciples were, "Peace be unto you." (John 20:19.) He has also promised: "Peace in this world, and eternal life in the world to come." (D&C 59:23.) The atonement and the resurrection have taken place. Our Lord and Savior suffered that appalling agony in Gethsemane. He performed the ultimate sacrifice in dying on the cross and then breaking the bonds of death.

All of us benefit from the transcendent blessings of the atonement and the resurrection, through which the divine healing process can work in our lives. The hurt can be replaced by the joy the Savior promised. To the doubting Thomas, Jesus said, "Be not faithless, but believing." (John 20:27.) Through faith and righteousness all of the inequities, injuries, and pains of this life can be fully compensated for and made right. Blessings denied in this life will be fully recompensed in the eternities. Through complete repentance of our sins we can be forgiven and we can enjoy eternal life. Thus our suffering in this life can be as the refining fire, purifying us for a higher purpose. Heartaches can be healed, and we can come to know a soul-satisfying joy and happiness beyond our dreams and expectations.

The resolution promised by the atonement and the resurrection continues in eternity. Physical limitations will be compensated. Alma's words are comforting: "The soul shall be restored to the body, and the body to the soul; yea, and every limb and joint shall be restored to its body; yea, even a hair of the head shall not be lost; but all things shall be restored to their proper and perfect frame." (Alma 40:23.)

The resolution is brought about by the Savior's intercession. As He said in the great intercessory prayer found in the seventeenth chapter of John, "And this is life eternal, that they might know thee the only true God, and Jesus Christ, whom thou hast sent." (John 17:3.) Then the Savior prayed for his apostles and all of the saints, saying, "I pray not for the world, but for them which thou hast given me; for they are thine. And all mine are thine, and thine are mine; and I am glorified in them." (John 17:9–10.)

All of us have made wrong turns along the way. I believe the kind and merciful God, whose children we are, will judge us as lightly as he can for the wrongs that we have done and give us the maximum blessing for the good that we do. Alma's sublime utterance seems to me an affirmation of this. Said Alma, "And not many days hence the Son of God shall come in his glory; and his glory shall be the glory of the Only Begotten of the Father, full of grace, equity, and truth, full of patience, mercy, and long-suffering, quick to hear the cries of his people and to answer their prayers." (Alma 9:26.)

Of vital importance is resolving transgression, experiencing the healing process which comes of repentance. As President Kimball reminds us, "The principle of repentance—of rising again whenever we fall, brushing ourselves off, and setting off again on that upward trail—is the basis for our hope. It is through repentance that the Lord Jesus Christ can work his healing miracle, infusing us with strength when we are weak, health when we are sick, hope when we are downhearted, love when we feel empty, and understanding when we search for truth." (*The Teachings of Spencer W. Kimball,* ed. Edward L. Kimball [Salt Lake City: Bookcraft, 1982], p. 106.)

One of the tender stories of the Book of Mormon takes place when Alma speaks to his son Corianton, who had fallen into transgression while on a mission to the Zoramites. As he counsels him to forsake his sin and turn again to the Lord, he learns that Corianton is worried about what will happen to him in the resurrection. There follows a detailed treatment of the probationary state of this life, of justice versus mercy, and God's plan for our happiness in the hereafter, culminating in this verse:

"And mercy claimeth the penitent, and mercy cometh because of the atonement; and the atonement bringeth to pass the resurrection of the dead; and the resurrection of the dead bringeth back men into the presence of God; and thus they are restored into his presence, to be judged according to their works, according to the law and justice." (Alma 42:23.)

The Savior gives us a profound key by which we can cope with and even surmount the debilitating forces of the world. Said the Savior, "I pray not that thou shouldest take them out of the world, but that thou shouldest keep them from the evil." (John 17:15.) This grand key then is that, regardless of the saturation of wickedness around us, we must stay free from the evil of the world. The Savior's prayer both commands us to avoid evil and proffers divine help to do so. Through this effort we become one with our Lord. The prayer of the Savior in Gethsemane was "That they all may be one; as thou, Father, art in me, and I in thee, that they also may be one in us: that the world may believe that thou hast sent me." (John 17:21.)

To remain true and faithful through this mortal veil of tears, we must love God with all our heart, might, mind, and strength and love our neighbor as ourselves. We must also stand together as families; as members of wards and branches, stakes and districts; and as a people. To our neighbors not of our faith we should be as the good Samaritan who cared for the man who fell among thieves. (See Luke 10:29–37.) We must gather strength from each other. We must also "succor the weak, lift up the hands which hang down, and strengthen the feeble knees." (D&C 81:5.)

Paul taught well on this subject. Said he to the Corinthians, speaking of the body or church of Christ: "That there should be no schism in the body; but that the members should have the same care one for another. And whether one member suffer, all the members suffer with it; or one member be honoured, all the members rejoice with it. Now ye are the body of Christ, and members in particular." (1 Cor. 12:25–27.) In this way, as individuals and as a people we may be kept from evil. As we go through travail and difficulty we may feel sorry for ourselves and despair, but with the love of God and the Saints, unitedly bearing each other's burdens, we can be happy and overcome evil.

Some faithful women have been denied that which is at the very center of their souls. In the eternal plan, no blessing will be kept from the faithful. No woman should question how the Savior values womanhood. The grieving Mary Magdalene was the first to visit the sepulchre after the crucifixion, and when she saw that the stone had been rolled away and that the tomb was empty, she ran to tell Peter and John. The two Apostles came to see and then went away sorrowing. But Mary stayed. She had stood near the cross. (See Matt. 27:56; Mark 15:40; John 19:25.) She had been at the burial. (See Matt. 27:61; Mark 15:47.) And now she stood weeping by the empty sepulchre. (See John 20:11.) There she was honored to be the first mortal to see the risen Lord. After He said, "Woman, why weepest thou?" she was instructed by Him: "Go to my brethren, and say unto them, I ascend unto my Father, and your Father; and to my God, and your God." (See John 20:15, 17.)

During His mortal ministry, Jesus left Judea to go to Galilee. He arrived at Jacob's well thirsty and weary from traveling. A woman of Samaria came to draw water. Jewish convention at the time forbade dealings with Samaritans. Yet "Jesus saith unto her, Give me to drink. . . .

"Then saith the woman of Samaria unto him, How is it that thou, being a Jew, askest drink of me, which am a woman of Samaria? . . .

"Jesus answered and said unto her, If thou knewest the gift of God, and who it is that saith to thee, Give me to drink; thou wouldest have asked of him, and he would have given thee living water."

Jesus went on to teach her about the living water "springing up into everlasting life." The Samaritan woman responded, "Sir, I perceive that thou art a prophet." Then she "saith unto him, I know that Messias cometh, which is called Christ: when he is come, he will tell us all things." At this point, Jesus revealed His true identity to her: "I that speak unto thee am he." (John 4:7–10, 14, 19, 25, 26.)

The resurrection and the atonement of the Savior can be a constant fortifying influence in our lives as illustrated by the account of Elizabeth Jackson, a pioneer in the Martin Handcart Company. She tells of the death of her husband, Aaron, on the Wyoming plains in 1856 in these moving words:

> About nine o'clock I retired. Bedding had become very scarce so I did not disrobe. I slept until, as it appeared to me, about midnight. I was extremely cold. The weather was bitter. I listened to hear if my husband breathed, he lay so still. I could not hear him. I became alarmed. I put my hand on

his body, when to my horror I discovered that my worst fears were confirmed. My husband was dead. I called for help to the other inmates of the tent. They could render me no aid; and there was no alternative but to remain alone by the side of the corpse till morning. Oh, how the dreary hours drew their tedious length along. When daylight came, some of the male part of the company prepared the body for burial. And oh, such a burial and funeral service. They did not remove his clothing—he had but little. They wrapped him in a blanket and placed him in a pile with thirteen others who had died, then covered him up with snow. The ground was frozen so hard that they could not dig a grave. He was left there to sleep in peace until the trump of God shall sound, and the dead in Christ shall awake and come forth in the morning of the first resurrection. We shall then again unite our hearts and lives, and eternity will furnish us with life forever more. (LeRoy R. and Ann W. Hafen, *Handcarts to Zion* [Glendale, California: The Arthur H. Clark Company, 1976], p. 111.)

To the question "Woman, why weepest thou?" we turn to the comforting words written to the faithful saints by John in the Book of Revelation:

"These are they which came out of great tribulation, and have washed their robes, and made them white in the blood of the Lamb.

"Therefore are they before the throne of God, and serve him day and night in his temple: and he that sitteth on the throne shall dwell among them.

"They shall hunger no more, neither thirst any more; neither shall the sun light on them, nor any heat.

"For the Lamb which is in the midst of the throne shall feed them, and shall lead them unto living fountains of waters: and God shall wipe away all tears from their eyes." (Rev. 7:14–17.)

To the question "Woman, why weepest thou?" I testify of the

great atoning sacrifice and breaking of the bonds of death by the Lord Jesus Christ, which shall indeed wipe away our tears. I have a witness of this. It has been given by the Holy Spirit of God.

I also testify that the Lord Jesus Christ is the head of this Church today. We see His omnipotent hand guiding this holy work. I further testify to the prophetic calling and great leadership of President Gordon B. Hinckley as His servant under whose inspired direction we are all privileged to serve.

I pray, as did King Benjamin, that we shall "be steadfast and immovable, always abounding in good works, that Christ, the Lord God Omnipotent, may seal [us] his, that [we] may be brought to heaven, that [we] may have everlasting salvation and eternal life, through the wisdom, and power, and justice, and mercy of him who created all things, in heaven and in earth, who is God above all." (Mosiah 5:15.)

President James E. Faust was called as a General Authority in 1972, was ordained an Apostle in 1978, and was sustained as a member of the First Presidency of the Church in 1995.

THE JOY OF HOPE FULFILLED

ELDER M. RUSSELL BALLARD

Living in these difficult times requires each one of us to main-tain a positive, hopeful perspective about the future. Today, more so than in the past, I am asked about the signs of the times and if I think the end of the world is near. My answer is the same one that Jesus gave some two thousand years ago: "But of that day and that hour knoweth no man, no, not the angels which are in heaven, neither the Son, but the Father. Take ye heed, watch and pray: for ye know not when the time is." (Mark 13:32–33.)

When Jesus was asked about the sign of His coming, he said: "Ye shall hear of wars and rumours of wars: *see that ye be not troubled: for all these things must come to pass,* but the end is not yet. For nation shall rise against nation, and kingdom against kingdom: and there shall be famines, and pestilences, and earth-quakes, in divers places. All these are the beginning of sorrows." (Matt. 24:6–8; italics added.)

Although the prophecies tell us that these things are to take place, more and more people are expressing great alarm at what appears to be an acceleration of worldwide calamity. As mem-bers of the Church, we must not forget the Savior's admonition: "Be not troubled: for all these things must come to pass." These are difficult times, when the forces of nature seem to be unleash-ing a flood of "famines, and pestilences, and earthquakes, in divers places."

127

Recently, I read a newspaper article that cited statistics from the U.S. Geological Survey indicating that earthquakes around the world are increasing in frequency and intensity. According to the article, only two major earthquakes (earthquakes measuring at least six on the Richter scale) occurred during the 1920s. In the 1930s the number increased to five, and then it decreased to four during the 1940s. But in the 1950s, nine major earthquakes occurred, followed by fifteen during the 1960s, forty-six during the 1970s, and fifty-two during the 1980s. Already [as of 1992] almost as many major earthquakes have occurred during the 1990s as during the entire decade of the 1980s.

The world is experiencing violent disorders, both physical and social. Here in the United States we are still reeling from two incredibly destructive hurricanes. People in the Philippines see no end to the devastation of the volcanic eruption of Mount Pinatubo. Famine grips portions of Africa, where tragic human suffering is prevalent. To a lesser degree, hunger afflicts millions, even in countries that have a high standard of living.

Political unrest, warfare, and economic chaos prevail in many parts of the world, and the plagues of pornography, drug misuse, immorality, AIDS, and child abuse become more oppressive with each passing day. The media busily satisfies an apparently insatiable appetite of audiences to witness murder, violence, nudity, sex, and profanity. Is not this the day of which Moroni spoke when he recorded: "Behold, I speak unto you as if ye were present, and yet ye are not. But behold, Jesus Christ hath shown you unto me, and I know your doing." (Morm. 8:35.) And then he prophesied of conditions of the world as they are today.

Whether or not these are indeed the last days or even "the beginning of sorrows" as the Savior foretold, some of us may find our lives laden with frustration, disappointment, and sorrow. Many feel helpless to deal with the chaos that seems to prevail in the world. Others anguish over family members who are being carried downstream in a swift, raging current of weakening values and declining moral standards. Children particularly are suffering as society drifts further and further away from the commandments of God.

Many have even resigned themselves to accept the wickedness and cruelty of the world as being irreparable. They have given up hope. They have decided to quit trying to make the world a better place in which they and their families can live. They have surrendered to despair.

Admittedly, we have ample reason to be deeply concerned because we see no immediate answers to the seemingly unsolvable problems confronting the human family. But regardless of this dark picture, which will ultimately get worse, we must never allow ourselves to give up hope! Moroni, having seen our day, counseled, "Wherefore, there must be faith; and if there must be faith there must also be hope." (Moro. 10:20.)

To all who have harbored feelings of despair and an absence of hope, I offer the words of the Lord through the Prophet Joseph Smith: "Fear not, little flock; do good; let earth and hell combine against you, for if ye are built upon my rock, they cannot prevail. . . . Look unto me in every thought; doubt not, fear not" (D&C 6:34, 36); "even so am I in the midst of you" (D&C 6:32).

My message to you is simply this: the Lord is in control. He knows the end from the beginning. He has given us adequate instruction that, if followed, will see us safely through any crisis. His purposes will be fulfilled, and someday we will understand the eternal reasons for all of these events. Therefore, today we must be careful not to overreact, nor should we be caught up in extreme preparations, but what we must do is keep the commandments of God and never lose hope!

But where do we find hope in the midst of such turmoil and

catastrophe? Quite simply, our one hope for spiritual safety during these turbulent times is to turn our minds and our hearts to Jesus Christ. The prophet Mormon taught: "Ye shall have hope through the atonement of Christ and the power of his resurrection, to be raised unto life eternal, and this because of your faith in him according to the promise. Wherefore, if a man have faith he must needs have hope; for without faith there cannot be any hope." (Moro. 7:41–42.)

Faith in God and in His Son, Jesus Christ, is absolutely essential for us to maintain a balanced perspective through times of trial and difficulty. Remember, nothing will occur in our lives that He does not understand. Alma taught, "And he shall go forth, suffering pains and afflictions and temptations of every kind; and this that the word might be fulfilled which saith he will take upon him the pains and the sicknesses of his people." (Alma 7:11.)

Please turn to Him if you are discouraged and struggling for direction in your life. Armed with the shield of faith, we can overcome many of our daily challenges and overpower our greatest weaknesses and fears, knowing that if we do our best to keep the commandments of God, come what may, we will be all right.

Of course, that does not necessarily mean that we will be spared personal suffering and heartache. Righteousness has never precluded adversity. But faith in the Lord Jesus Christ—real faith, whole-souled and unshakable—is a power to be reckoned with in the universe. It can be a causative force through which miracles are wrought. Or it can be a source of inner strength through which we find peace, comfort, and the courage to cope.

As we put our faith and trust to work, hope is born. Hope grows out of faith and gives meaning and purpose to all that we do. It can even give us the peaceful assurance we need to live happily in a world that is ripe with iniquity, calamity, and injustice.

As the end of the Savior's mortal ministry drew near, He offered this reassuring hope to His beloved disciples: "Peace I leave with you, my peace I give unto you: not as the world giveth, give I unto you. Let not your heart be troubled, neither let it be afraid." (John 14:27.)

Hope is a precious principle by which to live. However, some among us may have lost all hope because of sin and transgression. A person can become so deeply immersed in the ways of the world that he sees no way out and loses all hope. My plea to all who have fallen into this trap of the adversary is to never give up! Regardless of how desperate things may seem or how desperate they may yet become, please believe me, you can always have hope. Always.

Recently I had the privilege of performing the temple sealing ordinances for a wonderful family. It was a beautiful occasion, as such ceremonies almost always are. But if you had known the father of this family several years earlier, you would have understood what a miracle was taking place in the House of the Lord that day. With his permission I quote from a letter he wrote to me:

> I was born into the Church and was taught the gospel at my mother's knee. Through her diligence and perseverance, she kindled a small ember of testimony that never left me even through some of the roughest times of my life. In my teen years Satan hit me hard. It was during the late 1960s and early 1970s, a time of great turmoil, and Satan was hard at work on me. I was taken with the practice of free drugs, free love, free fun, and the rest of the world be damned. Beginning with my first drink of alcohol, I began to slowly deteriorate. After alcohol, other drugs were that much easier to use. In order to take drugs, you must become

131

a good liar. You learn to do whatever it takes to conceal your behavior from others.

After many years of living this way, all my moral fiber seemed to be completely eroded away. I had a minimal amount of conscience and had sunk to the depths of despair and depression. I watched friends die from drugs and suicide. As time passed, my friends and I were exposed to the criminal justice system. In fact, many of my former friends are still in prison. Had it not been for the small flicker of testimony instilled in me by my mother when I was a child, to know that Heavenly Father could still love me, I have reservations as to whether I would even be writing this letter today.

Some parents might have given up hope on this prodigal son, but not this man's mother. She continued to believe that he would find his way back to the teachings of his childhood and once again place his trust in the Lord Jesus Christ. With the loving support of his family and friends, that is exactly what he did. Let me read again from his letter:

"If there is one thing I have learned, it is that no matter how lost you feel, no matter how low you may have sunk, there can be forgiveness and peace. I learned that the further one drifts from the Lord, the harder it is to return to Him and His teachings. But once I opened my heart and called out in prayer to Heavenly Father to help me in the name of His Son, Jesus Christ, I came to know the power of repentance and the blessings of obedience to God's commandments."

I wish all of you could have been with us in the temple that day to feel the joy of hope fulfilled. I am sure you would have sensed, as I did, the rekindled love for God and the sublime happiness that filled the heart of my friend's mother as her four sons, their companions, and other family members surrounded her in the sealing room.

The Apostle Paul taught that three divine principles form a

foundation upon which we can build the structure of our lives. They are faith, hope, and charity. (See 1 Cor. 13:13.) Together they give us a base of support like the legs of a three-legged stool. Each principle is significant within itself, but each also plays an important supporting role. Each is incomplete without the others. Hope helps faith develop. Likewise, true faith gives birth to hope. When we begin to lose hope, we are faltering also in our measure of faith. The principles of faith and hope working together must be accompanied by charity, which is the greatest of all. According to Mormon, "charity is the pure love of Christ, and it endureth forever." (Moro. 7:47.) It is the perfect manifestation of our faith and hope.

Working together, these three eternal principles will help give us the broad eternal perspective we need to face life's toughest challenges, including the prophesied ordeals of the last days. Real faith fosters hope for the future; it allows us to look beyond ourselves and our present cares. Fortified by hope, we are moved to demonstrate the pure love of Christ through daily acts of obedience and Christian service.

I assure you that our Heavenly Father is aware of us, individually and collectively. He understands the spiritual, physical, and emotional difficulties we face in the world today. In fact, they are all part of His plan for our eternal growth and development. And His promise to us is sure: "He that endureth in faith and doeth my will, the same shall overcome." (D&C 63:20.)

The Savior promised that "no weapon that is formed against thee shall prosper. . . . This is the heritage of the servants of the Lord." (3 Ne. 22:17.)

May we all find the "peace of God, which passeth all understanding" (Philip. 4:7), which can be found only through charity, faith, and hope.

May I share with you my testimony that I know that the

133

Lord Jesus Christ lives. He has restored His Church to the earth through the Prophet Joseph Smith. Our assurance of eternal life rests in our love of God and the keeping of His commandments. This knowledge gives me hope and faith. May it be so with each of you, I humbly pray.

Elder M. Russell Ballard was called as a General Authority in 1976, and was ordained an Apostle in 1985.

DO NOT DESPAIR

P R E S I D E N T   E Z R A   T A F T   B E N S O N

We live in an age when, as the Lord foretold, men's hearts are failing them, not only physically but in spirit. (See D&C 45:26.) Many are giving up heart for the battle of life. Suicide ranks as a major cause of the deaths to college students. As the showdown between good and evil approaches with its accompanying trials and tribulations, Satan is increasingly striving to overcome the Saints with despair, discouragement, despondency, and depression.

Yet, of all people, we as Latter-day Saints should be the most optimistic and the least pessimistic. For while we know that "peace shall be taken from the earth, and the devil shall have power over his own dominion," we are also assured that "the Lord shall have power over his saints, and shall reign in their midst." (D&C 1:35–36.)

With the assurance that the Church shall remain intact with God directing it through the troubled times ahead, it then becomes our individual responsibility to see that each of us remains faithful to the Church and its teachings. "He that remaineth steadfast and is not overcome, the same shall be saved." (JS–M 1:11.) To help us from being overcome by the devil's designs of despair, discouragement, depression, and despondency, the Lord has provided at least a dozen ways which, if followed, will lift our spirits and send us on our way rejoicing.

135

First, repentance. In the Book of Mormon we read that "despair cometh because of iniquity." (Moro. 10:22.) "When I do good I feel good," said Abraham Lincoln, "and when I do bad I feel bad." Sin pulls a man down into despondency and despair. While a man may take some temporary pleasure in sin, the end result is unhappiness. "Wickedness never was happiness." (Al. 41:10.) Sin creates disharmony with God and is depressing to the spirit. Therefore, a man would do well to examine himself to see that he is in harmony with all of God's laws. Every law kept brings a particular blessing. Every law broken brings a particular blight. Those who are heavy laden with despair should come unto the Lord, for his yoke is easy and his burden is light. (See Matt. 11:28–30.)

Second, prayer. Prayer in the hour of need is a great boon. From simple trials to our Gethsemanes, prayer can put us in touch with God, our greatest source of comfort and counsel. "Pray always, that you may come off conqueror" (D&C 10:5)— persistent prayer. "Exerting all my powers to call upon God to deliver me" is how the young Joseph Smith describes the method which he used in the Sacred Grove to keep the adversary from destroying him. (JS–H 1:16.) This is also a key to use in keeping depression from destroying us.

Third, service. To lose yourself in righteous service to others can lift your sights and get your mind off personal problems or at least put them in proper focus. "When you find yourselves a little gloomy," said President Lorenzo Snow, "look around you and find somebody that is in a worse plight than yourself; go to him and find out what the trouble is, then try to remove it with the wisdom which the Lord bestows upon you; and the first thing you know, your gloom is gone, you feel light, the Spirit of the Lord is upon you, and everything seems illuminated." (Conference Report, 6 Apr. 1899, pp. 2–3.)

A woman whose life is involved in the righteous rearing of

her children has a better chance of keeping up her spirits than the woman whose total concern is centered in her own personal problems.

Fourth, work. The earth was cursed for Adam's sake. Work is our blessing, not our doom. God has a work to do, and so should we. Retirement from work has depressed many a man and hastened his death. It has been said that even the very fiends weave ropes of sand rather than to face the pure hell of idleness. We should work at taking care of the spiritual, mental, social, and physical needs of ourselves and those whom we are charged to help. In the church of Jesus Christ there is plenty of work to do to move forward the kingdom of God. Every member a missionary, family genealogy and temple work, home evenings, receiving a Church assignment and magnifying it are but a few of our required labors.

Fifth, health. The condition of the physical body can affect the spirit. That's why the Lord gave us the Word of Wisdom. He also said that we should retire to our beds early and arise early (see D&C 88:124), that we should not run faster than we have strength (see D&C 10:4), and that we should use moderation in all good things. In general, the more food we eat in its natural state and the less it is refined without additives, the healthier it will be for us. Food can affect the mind, and deficiencies in certain elements in the body can promote mental depression. A good physical examination periodically is a safeguard and may spot problems that can he remedied. Rest and physical exercise are essential, and a walk in the fresh air can refresh the spirit. Wholesome recreation is part of our religion, and a change of pace is necessary, and even its anticipation can lift the spirit.

Sixth, reading. Many a man in his hour of trial has turned to the Book of Mormon and been enlightened, enlivened, and comforted.

The psalms in the Old Testament have a special food for the

soul of one in distress. In our day we are blessed with the Doctrine and Covenants, modern revelation. The words of the prophets, particularly the living president of the Church, are crucial reading and can give direction and comfort in an hour when one is down.

Seventh, blessing. In a particularly stressful time, or in the anticipation of a critical event, one can seek for a blessing under the hands of the priesthood. Even the Prophet Joseph Smith sought and received a blessing under the hands of Brigham Young and received solace and direction for his soul. Fathers, so live that you can bless your own wives and children. To receive, and then consistently and prayerfully ponder, one's patriarchal blessing can give helpful insight, particularly in an hour of need. The sacrament will "bless . . . the souls" (D&C 20:77, 79) of all those who worthily partake of it, and as such it should be taken often, even by the bedfast.

Eighth, fasting. A certain kind of devil goes not out except by fasting and prayer, the scripture tells us. (See Matt. 17:21.) Periodic fasting can help clear up the mind and strengthen the body and the spirit. The usual fast, the one we are asked to participate in for fast Sunday, is for 24 hours without food or drink. Some people, feeling the need, have gone on longer fasts of abstaining from food but have taken the needed liquids. Wisdom should be used, and the fast should be broken with light eating. To make a fast most fruitful, it should be coupled with prayer and meditation; physical work should be held to a minimum, and it's a blessing if one can ponder on the scriptures and the reason for the fast.

Ninth, friends. The fellowship of true friends who can hear you out, share your joys, help carry your burdens, and correctly counsel you is priceless. For one who has been in the prison of depression, the words of the Prophet Joseph Smith have special meaning when he said, "How sweet the voice of a friend is; one

138

token of friendship from any source whatever awakens and calls into action every sympathetic feeling." (*Teachings of the Prophet Joseph Smith,* p. 134.)

Ideally, your family ought to be your closest friends. Most important, we should seek to become the friend of our Father in heaven and our brother Jesus the Christ. What a boon to be in the company of those who edify you. To have friends, one should be friendly. Friendship should begin at home and then be extended to encompass the home teacher, quorum leader, bishop, and other Church teachers and leaders. To meet often with the Saints and enjoy their companionship can buoy up the heart.

Tenth, music. Inspiring music may fill the soul with heavenly thoughts, move one to righteous action, or speak peace to the soul. When Saul was troubled with an evil spirit, David played for him with his harp and Saul was refreshed and the evil spirit departed. (See 1 Sam. 16:23.) Elder Boyd K. Packer has wisely suggested memorizing some of the inspiring songs of Zion and then, when the mind is afflicted with temptations, to sing aloud, to keep before your mind the inspiring words and thus crowd out the evil thoughts. (See *Ensign,* Jan. 1924, p. 28.) This could also be done to crowd out debilitating, depressive thoughts.

Eleventh, endurance. When George A. Smith was very ill, he was visited by his cousin, the Prophet Joseph Smith. The afflicted man reported: "He [the Prophet] told me I should never get discouraged, whatever difficulties might surround me. If I were sunk into the lowest pit of Nova Scotia and all the Rocky Mountains piled on top of me, I ought not to be discouraged, but hang on, exercise faith, and keep up good courage, and I should come out on the top of the heap." (*George A. Smith Family,* comp. Zora Smith Jarvis [Provo, Utah: Brigham Young University Press, 1962], p. 54.)

There are times when you simply have to righteously hang on and outlast the devil until his depressive spirit leaves you. As the Lord told the Prophet Joseph Smith: "Thine adversity and thine afflictions shall be but a small moment; And then, if thou endure it well, God shall exalt thee on high." (D&C 121:7–8.)

To press on in noble endeavors, even while surrounded by a cloud of depression, will eventually bring you out on top into the sunshine. Even our master Jesus the Christ, while facing that supreme test of being temporarily left alone by our Father during the crucifixion, continued performing his labors for the children of men, and then shortly thereafter he was glorified and received a fulness of joy. While you are going through your trial, you can recall your past victories and count the blessings that you do have with a sure hope of greater ones to follow if you are faithful. And you can have that certain knowledge that in due time God will wipe away all tears and that "eye hath not seen, nor ear heard, neither have entered into the heart of man, the things which God hath prepared for them that love him." (1 Cor. 2:9.)

And twelfth, goals. Every accountable child of God needs to set goals, short- and long-range goals. A man who is pressing forward to accomplish worthy goals can soon put despondency under his feet, and once a goal is accomplished, others can be set up. Some will be continuing goals. Each week when we partake of the sacrament we commit ourselves to the goals of taking upon ourselves the name of Christ, of always remembering him and keeping his commandments. Of Jesus' preparation for his mission, the scripture states that he "increased in wisdom and stature, and in favour with God and man." (Luke 2:52.) This encompasses four main areas for goals: spiritual, mental, physical, and social. "Therefore, what manner of men ought ye to be?" asked the Master, and he answered, "Verily I say unto you, even as I am." (3 Ne. 27:27.) Now there is a lifetime goal—to walk in his steps, to perfect ourselves in every virtue as he has done, to seek his face, and to work to make our calling and election sure.

"Brethren," said Paul, " . . . this one thing I do, forgetting those things which are behind, and reaching forth unto those things which are before, I press toward the mark for the prize of the high calling of God in Christ Jesus." (Philip. 3:13–14.)

Let your minds be filled with the goal of being like the Lord, and you will crowd out depressing thoughts as you anxiously seek to know him and do his will. "Let this mind be in you," said Paul. (Philip. 2:5.) "Look unto me in every thought," said Jesus. (D&C 6:36.) And what will follow if we do? "Thou wilt keep him in perfect peace, whose mind is stayed on thee." (Isa. 26:3.)

"Salvation," said the Prophet Joseph Smith, "is nothing more nor less than to triumph over all our enemies and put them under our feet." (*Teachings of the Prophet Joseph Smith,* p. 297.) We can rise above the enemies of despair, depression, discouragement, and despondency by remembering that God provides righteous alternatives, some of which I have mentioned. As it states in the Bible, "There hath no temptation taken you but such as is common to man: but God is faithful, who will not suffer you to be tempted above that ye are able; but will with the temptation also make a way to escape, that ye may be able to bear it." (1 Cor. 10:13.)

Yes, life is a test; it is a probation; and perhaps being away from our heavenly home we feel sometimes, as holy men in the past have felt, that "they were strangers and pilgrims on the earth." (See D&C 45:13.)

Some of you will recall in that great book *Pilgrim's Progress* by John Bunyan that the main character known as Christian was trying to press forward to gain entrance to the celestial city. He made it to his goal, but in order to do so, he had to overcome many obstacles, one of which was to escape from the Giant Despair. To lift our spirit and send us on our way rejoicing, the devil's designs of despair, discouragement, depression, and despondency can be defeated in a dozen ways, namely: repentance, prayer, service, work, health, reading, blessings, fasting, friends, music, endurance, and goals.

May we use them all in the difficult days ahead so that we Christian pilgrims will have greater happiness here and go on to a fulness of joy in the highest realms of the celestial kingdom.

President Ezra Taft Benson was ordained an Apostle in 1943, was sustained President of the Church in 1985, and died in 1994.

INDEX